EMPTYING THE SOUL FROM A TO Z

WITH A TWIST OF POETRY

BY UGANDA REED

COPYRIGHT © 2008 by UGANDA REED

ALL RIGHTS RESERVED. THIS BOOK IS PROTECTED UNDER THE COPYRIGHT LAWS OF THE UNITED STATES OF AMERICA. THIS BOOK MAY NOT BE COPIED OR REPRINTED FOR COMMERCIAL PROFIT OR GAIN. NO PART OF THIS BOOK MAY BE REPRODUCED, STORED IN A RETRIEVAL SYSTEM, OR TRANSMITTED BY ANY MEANS WITHOUT THE WRITTEN PERMISSION OF THE PUBLISHER/AUTHOR. THE USE OF SOME QUOTATIONS OR PAGES MAY BE USED WITH PRIOR PERMISSION. UNLESS OTHERWISE IDENTIFIED, SCRIPTURE QUOTATIONS ARE FROM THE KING JAMES VERSON OF THE BIBLE.

MAKE AWARE OF THE CAPITALIZATIONS IN THIS BOOK. THE WORD'S CONNECTIED TO THE ENEMY'S CAMP IS NOT CAPITALIZED. I CHOSE NOT TO GIVE HIM ENERGY, EVEN WITH THE VIOLATION OF THE GRAMMATICAL RULES.

U. R. LIFE
P.O BOX 392554
SNELLVILLE, GA 30039-0043
gmillions122@yahoo.com

"AND THE LORD GOD FORMED MAN OF THE DUST OF THE GROUND, AND BREATHED INTO HIS NOSTRILS <u>THE BREATH OF LIFE</u>; AND MAN BECAME A LIVING BEING." GENESIS 2VS7

ISBN: 978-0-6152-0426-0

THIS BOOK IS A WORK OF NON-FICTION. UNLESS OTHERWISE NOTED, THE AUTHOR AND PUBLISHER MAKE NO EXPLICIT GUARANTEES AS TO THE ACCURACY OF

THIS BOOK IS PRINTED ON ACID-FREE PAPER.

"I FOUND MYSELF PRESSING TOWARD MY DESTINY, FIGHTING THROUGH ADVERSITIES, ONLY TO REALIZE DESTINY HAD PRESSED ITS WAY TOWARD ME."

By: UGANDA

DEDICATION

TO MY FATHER IN HEAVEN THANK YOU FOR ALLOWING ME TO FIND YOU IN ME, FOR LEAVING ME SOMETHING INSIDE THAT REFUSED TO GIVE UP! THANKS FOR MY TRIALS, MY PAINS, MY SUFFERING AND FOR YOUR LOVE. THANKS FOR NOT LETTING IT BE TOO LATE TO BE EMPTIED OUT AND GIVING ME TIME TO BECOME FILLED WITH THE HOLY SPIRIT.

TO MY CHILDREN I HAVE ALWAYS THANKED GOD FOR CHOOSING ME TO BE THE ONE THAT GAVE YOU LIFE AND TO SPEAK LIFE INTO YOU. I WANT TO THANK YOU FOR YOUR UNDERSTANDING, EVEN IN OUR STRUGGLES TOGETHER!

TO MYSELF THANKS FOR NEVER GIVING UP AND FOR HOLDING ON FOR DEAR LIFE UNTIL THE RELEASE CAME. THANKS FOR FIGHTING FOR ME! THANKS FOR SEEKING THE KINGDOM FOR YOU HAVE NOW BEEN CROWNED A KINGDOMS CHILD! THANKS FOR EMPTYING ALL OF YESTERDAY SO THAT WE CAN LIVE IN TODAY AND FOR ETERNITY. I LOVE YOU!!!!!!!!!!!!

ACKNOWLEDGMENTS

FROM THE DEPTHS OF MY SOUL WHERE HE FOUND ME I THANK MY MASTER, MY CREATOR, MY SOURCE, AND MY SUPPLIER! HE IS ALPHA AND OMEGA THE BEGINNING AND THE END. HE IS MIGHTY IN BATTLE! GOD YOU SAVED ME!

TO THE GIFTS GOD GAVE ME BY BIRTH CHELSIE, ALLEXIOUS, EZETRIS, DAMEEK AND STARRASIA WHO GOD GAVE TO ME TO LOVE AND HELP FIND HER WAY. YOU ARE THE LIGHTS TO EVERY PATHWAY IN FINDING MY DESTINY. THANKS FOR GIVING ME THE VISION TO SEE PAST THE HARD TIMES, THE FALLS, THE OBSTACLES AND THE TRIALS THAT GAVE ME STRENGTH TO NEVER GIVE UP. THANKS FOR TRUSTING ME TO LOVE AND LEAD YOU IN LIFE. THANKS FOR LOVING ME AND BELIEVING IN ME.

ALL MY ANGELS IN HIGH PLACES I LOVE YOU: (GRANDADDY & MY FATHER THANK YOU FOR WATCHING OVER ME FROM ABOVE.)
GRANDMOTHER SARAH AND DARRYL SEAY DUE TO THE LOSS OF THE TWO OF YOU SO CLOSE TOGETHER I LEARNED TO PRESS PAST THE SCARES OF LIFE AND FIND A PLACE OF PEACE EVEN IN THE MIST OF PAIN.

THANKS MOM FOR GIVING ME LIFE AND ALWAYS TELLING ME I CAN DO ANYTHING I PUT MY MIND TO. THANKS FOR ALWAYS HOLDING ON EVEN THROUGH THE PAIN AND VALLEYS LOW. YOU TAUGHT ME HOW TO BE TOUGH EVEN IN YOUR AFFLICTIONS! ONLY YOU CAN STOP THE RAIN!

MY TWO SISTERS AND TWO BROTHERS WE HAVE THE SAME SPIRIT TO NEVER GIVE UP DESPITE OUR ADVERSITIES. I LOVE YOU KEEP PRESSING! THE ENEMY ONLY FIGHTS HARD WHEN HE KNOWS YOU ARE CHOSEN.

TO MY SISTER LAYSHA THANKS FOR SEEING THE GOD FLOWING THROUGH ME AND ALLOWING ME TO KNOW YOU TRULY LOVE ME AND SEE ME AS YOUR ANGEL. I HOLD TEARS ON THE LETTERS I RECEIVED FROM YOU. GOD SAID

THAT LIFE LIES IN YOUR HANDS EMBRACE IT, LOVE IT, AND CONQUER IT. NOTHING CAN HOLD YOU DOWN BUT YOU!

TO ALL OF MY FAMILY MEMBERS: MY GRANDPARENTS, UNCLES, AUNTS, COUSINS, NIECES/NEPHEW I THANK GOD FOR ALLOWING US TO BE APART OF

THE SAME WORLDLY AND SPIRITUAL FAMILY! (A SPECIAL THANKS TO MY UNCLE J.M AND MY AUNTS ON MY MOTHER SIDE OF THE FAMILY) KNOW THAT LIFE ROADS ARE AS FAR AS YOU CAN SEE THEM KEEP YOUR EYES ON THE PRIZE! TRY GOD HE WILL NOT FAIL YOU! I LOVE ALL OF YOU FROM THE BOTTOM OF MY HEART TO THE DEPTHS OF MY SOUL!

TO ALL MY CLOSE FRIENDS AND MY WORLDLY ASSOCIATES ONLY GOD KNOWS WHY OUR ROADS CROSSED, BUT I THANK HIM! THANKS FOR EVERYTHING; THE GOOD, THE BAD, AND THE UGLY! FOR ALL MY CLOSE AND TRUE FRIENDS THANK YOU FOR BEING JUST THAT! GOD HAS A SEASON FOR EVRYTHING! YOUR SEASON IS COMING!

LIFE' I FOUND YOU AFTER DESTINY WALKED YOU RIGHT INTO ME, AND ALLOWED MY HEART TO BREATHE!

TO MYSELF THANK YOU FOR NOT GIVING UP WHEN TIMES SEEMED SO HARD, THANK YOU FOR GIVING UP EVERYTHING TO GAIN ETERNITY! I KNOW ROADS WHERE TOUGH BUT YOU MADE IT!

EVERYDAY IS A NEW BEGINNING! GOD'S BREATH IS STILL IN YOU!! JUMP GOD WILL CATCH YOU NO MATTER HOW DEEP YOU ARE, NO MATTER HOW FAR HE HAS TO GO TO CATCH YOU!!!! IT'S ALREADY DONE!!!

CONTENTS

Acknowledgements................... 7
Table of contents 9
My Introductions to Live Now...... 11

I. Am I who I am apart from Darkness:(A-D)   15

II. Emptying Me Out From the World:(E-H)   29

III. I am Cast Out Yet Unconquered: (I-L)   43

IV. Manifestation of the Pain: (M-P)   65

V. Questioning the fall of Babylon in Me: (Q-T)   91

VI. Understanding the Value of X: (U-X)   111

VII. Yesterdays Fighting Has to Stop
      "Then u can be Free": (Y-Z)   125

VIII. Who's Your Daddy Now?   135

IX. From A to Z Meditate…   143

INTRODUCTION

There's a lot of confusion going on inside of us. We subconsciously ask ourselves, when our life truly start! Where do we begin our destiny? How do we know we are moving in the right directions or if we are on the right path?

People come into our lives for a reason, a season and some even for a life time. How do we find out their purpose in our space? Sometimes I ask why I let them in my life to begin with. If it was up to me they would not have been allowed in my space. Even though they are here under false pretense they serve a purpose, rather we like it or not.

As years have past me by many have come and gone due to the realization that people pretend to be what I was looking for in a friend, lover, or companion, but as time passes I see the truth come out. I began to ask why I ever let that person in. There is a reason and it was up to me to find out their purpose in my life. In order to get out of that person what was placed there to help or make me grow I had to learn from that situation what I needed to move forward. I had to realize the spiritual lesson not the worldly pain, then I had to exit myself at the time my inner spirit said it was time to go. If we continue to stay in a place we have out grown or surpassed we will soon find ourselves in a dark hole searching for light because we have allowed them to darken our space and stop our growth. Their purpose has already been served! We allow them to out last the time God gave them in our lives!

Every one of us is a part of a spiritual body. We serve our own purpose. If we are not doing what it is we are called to do the body is unbalanced. Everyday we get up we move to our own pace without acknowledging our Creator, our protector, our guider, our master, and the source of our energy.

Why? Because we do not realize that the energy we use is connected to a higher power. That higher power connects us to people and higher places. He even connects us to our inner being. When we are not connected to the source and power we connect ourselves to the world and the world feeds us bad energy and contaminated resources. This indeed leads us to making the wrong decisions and questioning who we are. We are children of the most high! We are powerful beyond measures! We are a divine purpose designed to give to the world that which we were predestined to give. We are made in His image, equipped with everything we need to carry out our divine purpose. If we are ever to find out our true purpose we must first empty our souls from all the trash the world placed in us from A to Z. Once we empty our souls we will begin to find ourselves at a place where we can be filled with the love and power of our Creator which will allow our spirits to soar. Once we have found our inner spirit under the rebels of live we will begin to shift into a place where we can find our divine purpose. Once we find our divine purpose we meet up with destiny. Once we meet up with destiny we will begin to see a place of true prosperity.

I read in the Bible "you can not serve two masters; we will either despise one and love the other." My eyes loved the worldly things but I was blinded, lost and confused. Until one day I started pouring out tears from the bottom of my soul to the crowns within my mind. Pain began to be released; heart aches were no more, and everything that buried my soul beneath poured up out of me. There's a saying that says "Let go and let God!" I finally realized what that meant for my life when I found a place in me where I could allow God to set me free and guide me to my destiny.

When we find out and conquer our true fears then we can find ourselves and be comfortable with who we are. We have to love and acknowledge the good, the bad, and the ugly of what we have become in order to become what we were predestined to be so that others can also become set free. We become the light that shines even in darkness so that others can find their way back to the true place where they were proclaimed to be free.

I wanted to write my book in all caps but in order to touch as many people as possible I revised it for better reading purposes.

CAPITALIZING - Means affecting life; serious; chief, leading; excellent;

As you read you will find that the chapter pages are capitalized. I kept them capitalized to express the uniqueness of my life. Everything that happened to me in my life I have capitalized off of. I capitalized off my sorrows and my miseries, my loses and my gains, my heart aches and pains, my deaths that happened in my soul and everything that life has unfolded in front of me. I capitalized from it all.

By capitalizing I began to turn everything that was happening inside me into supply and demand. My pain was the supply and the anger was the demand. The very thing that was tearing me down caused me to see life as an experience. I became a new spectator for Christ. I realized that if I did not experience the things that were on my plate I would not have been able to make it through my worldly deaths and spiritual battles.

We have to capitalize off the things that to others may not seem to hold value but to ourselves that's all we have to hold on to. During those times we have to realize that if we do not expose ourselves the world will try to expose us. If or when the world exposes us, it's trying to destroy and take us down with the things we try to keep hidden. If we expose ourselves the world and no one else will have anything over us to take us down. We will hold the keys to our life's doors, not man.

We will then be able to walk this earth without ever feeling guilty, ashamed or misunderstood. People seem to already think they know who we are and how far we will have to climb to get to where we need to go. No one can judge our steps and have an accurate opinion except for the one who ordered them! All we need to do is realize people are going to talk, turn their backs on us, and look down on us; what will truly determine the outcome is our response to them and the situations. Our response is what will soon begin to define who we are. What we don't need to do is allow their words to hold weight in our mind. Mess the enemy up and free your mind/your soul!!

My grandmother used to tell me nothing from nothing, leaves nothing! You have to know you are something, if you weren't, the enemy would not be fighting you so hard. There would not be so much pain sent to try and take your crown if you weren't somebody. The world didn't give it to you and the world can't take it away! Empty your mind and take back what the enemy stole from you! It's waiting! God has it that means you still can get what ever you set your mind on.

**** I read something so powerful I would like to share it with you. This was written by an awesome man. This man stood on strength, faith and the knowledge of power even in his darkest moments. He alone should have shown us no matter what, we can still make it!

Our deepest fear is not that we are inadequate. Our deepest fear is that We are powerful beyond measures. It is our light, not our darkness, that most frightens us.
We ask ourselves, who am I to be brilliant, gorgeous, talented and fabulous? Actually, who are you not to be?
You are a child of God. Your playing small doesn't serve the world. There's nothing enlightened about shrinking so that other people won't feel insecure around you. We were born to make manifest the glory of God that is within us.
It's not just in some of us, it's in everyone. And as we let our own light shine, we unconsciously give others permission to do the same. As we are liberated from our own fear, our presence automatically liberates others…as spoken **by Nelson Mandela**

CHAPTER ONE

AM I who I AM APART FROM DARKNESS? (A-D)

"IT IS NOT DARKNESS THAT SCARES US IT IS OUR LIFE SHOWN IN THE LIGHT THAT BRINGS FEAR THAT WE'VE BEEN EXPOSED"

MY STORY WITH A TWIST OF POETRY

(AM I WHO I AM)

Am I who I am apart from darkness? I assume I am.
I was born with a silver spoon. Wealth and riches I knew.
My family all around me trying to keep me in the will of the greatest King, yet my mind had a different dream.
Growing up in church, my life full of unlimited dreams!
I had no clue it would soon be removed.
My mother and father in the same home building a house of prosperity for my sisters and me,
Oh how my father adored us and wanted us to have it all.
He decided to take a leave from this place he perceived would let him be all that he could be. Yet forced him into this dark place called streets where he soon became a self made king!
Not knowing the devil had it out for us, my father decided to live a life of lust. Leaving my mother with a decision to make which pushed her heart into more pain.
She began to hate the love she had for him and wanted it to disappear.
As time passed you could see a shift and it was clear; her mood had changed and life would never be the same.
Where was the love?
Mother and father was no more and we were out the door.
Now I am eight maybe nine who would have known that my heart would sing a sad love song. I didn't understand what was happening I just felt I was living in a bad dream. We were looking for a place to be, while they tore up our family.
To and from we were pitched till we landed in a ditch trying to recover from the storm, my mother ran into another man's arms!

Am I who I am? I asked myself. Apart from darkness I didn't know what was left. I was living in a place of make believe never realizing what's next for me. Often misunderstood never knew true love, so I gave to man what I knew; Pain!

Beneath the rubble there's pain making up the storm and rain in my life while I begin to fight.

I was fighting against the force of life trying not to destroy the little light in those walls around me, as I looked for a place of peace!

I couldn't sleep at night until quietness took flight; from the other room with the noise of defeat, pounding against flesh and destroying me. So, I looked outside my window, looking up to my one true hero (My Creator).

Asking Him "how do I ease this pain that a man made from the other room?" After seeing my mother bruises I knew the noise that kept me awake was his fist against her face.

Oh how I wondered was this life truly for me, was I meant to live in pain and misery.

Nine I was, trying to figure out this world. How do you go from riches to rags, is life really that sad?

In this house with a man, my best interest is not his plans. My mother could not see past his lies and deceit or how this man had it out for me.

He's not my father and showed he did not want to be so the enemy made his job secure. He used him to try and destroy the life God had for me as he continued to bring the pain in the mist of the catastrophe.

Blind my mother was thinking it was love. What love has to do with it when you are a woman with another man kids. It was up to her to teach us how to make it in this world being her little girls.

The man from the other room; kept her locked away and wish we would disappear so that he can create his own family.

Not knowing how to be a man of integrity, he had his own master plan you see; he teaching me was a part of the enemy plan to take me into captivity.

He was sent there to steal, kill and destroy the words God had spoken before my birth.

Always left alone to raise myself and care for those at home. I was sad and confused now feeling misused.

Am I who I am apart from darkness or do God have His own master plan that will start where I end at the iron wall within.

So innocent I seemed to be until the world captured me into a place of no man's land walking around with my own plan. So I had to say goodbye to that little girl that often cried from the pain that was being held within?

I had to bury that little girl beneath so that she would not continue to be defeated by the cruelty this world was throwing at me.

Which caused her to be bound in shackles and chains upon her feet from the weight of the streets; now being held down against her will, bound and taken over forced into the traps of flesh tasting the spirits death, becoming rubbish with nothing left but the streets.

No limits in the streets not even a second heart beat at the sound of trouble I continued to be taken over acting out from the pain of my mother's choices.

I was trying to ignore those voices from within yet begin to take life for a spin.

Oh no! Could it be that I can't let man love me! Scared of the empty hole that man made, when he dragged my mother across the pave in front of me! What do I do? So lost, so confused!

How can a man take from me the love in which I came from, could life ever feel so numb?

Am I who I am? I am who I am, I am a made woman by the streets at only sixteen, trying to determine who I be.

The pain made a bully which took away the God in me as I walked the halls and streets.

Straight A's in school, yet mean as could be trying to hide behind the pain and misery.

Rough and tough didn't take any stuff mean what I say on any given day.

Moving at a moments time all messed up on the inside, beautiful on the out all fixed up so the world would not see the mess I held inside of me.
I could not let anyone through so I hid behind the iron walls within and began to run the streets of sin.
The enemy took a stand moving to and fro knocking down and kicking in doors. He came to devour me with a great vengeance I now see; in the mist of my captivity in this world where I supposed to be free.
My eyes have seen what my mind could never be and things my heart did not want to keep.
Pushed into another test, oh God what's next?
You know your eyes tell their own story even when you've been taken under. But beyond the scene God knew what was next for me.
So I asked him, Am I who I am? Am I in your master plan?
I was defined by my flesh and not the God in me.
I Am who I am in God despite of what the world said or thought I would be!

(BECAUSE I AM WHO I AM)

Between the streets of life I did not stop without a fight. Backed into a corner I would come out on top with people wondering who Am I and what I Am about.
Once the world took over me it was hard to defeat the iron wall that stood up tall inside dead man's land. Couldn't be beaten already broken from the sound of my mother being choked from that man you know from that other room who himself is lost and confused.
He's smoked out, cracked out what could it be, lights out now I feel my mother needs me. The streets looked good for money when I had drug dealers around me wanting to know who I am so I began my own master plan!

Only a select few knew me for the streets, so laid back yet understood my life was in my hood.

It wasn't because of who I was or where I was from but because my environment took me under.

In my hood I saw many things, things I wish my eyes didn't see things that I tried to bury beneath. How can you solve mysteries of those that are already deceased inside my mind or where their bodies laid on the streets? I don't know yet my mind can't see.

My mind had seen so many harmful things. In trunks, even ovens if they didn't tell where the money was or other things that held value on the streets. In my mind I wasn't trying to promote catastrophe. I was just trying to feed those that were in need like me and my family.

Because I Am now who I Am the streets became my man, and many bad decisions I made acting out from the pain. Thinking it was alright to be what ever I saw fit to believe after all that church ran out of me. During the storm and rain I began to pain those that got close to me not knowing if they were real or make believe.

Due to the things my eyes had seen I couldn't let them near the heart that couldn't see through the clouds of misery. Time can only tell how much hell we will live in on earth until we fall back to the dust in which we came, or realize where we are from and claim the only true one. (My Creator)! At that moment I no longer understood so I was committed to man, that's the street you see it was calling for me.

All out of control feeling unloved and no arms to hold me so I began to snuggle in the arms of the wrong men, raped of who I wanted to be, degraded of my body. Leading me to something unplanned yet apart of me at the age of seventeen, something was growing inside me. Could I ever recover or will this also take me under.

(COULD I BE WHAT I AM)

Could I be pregnant at the age of seventeen and lost to the streets in the middle of a world of defeat? I must be I'm crying on the steps lying in my sister's lap not understanding how this happened to me already five months when I was told not ready to unfold what had captivated my soul. Courage could not save me no matter how much I had on the streets, this battle was no match for me for destiny had taken over and pushed me head first. This was not part of my plan, but God had his own master plan; which involved slowing me down to the streets.

To my mother I became her child held up in chains with shackles bounding my feet by the mess from the streets. Wrapped up over taken by the presence of life who is not giving up without a fight. Pushing me into a place where the streets needed to be erased in my mind as I conquered these mountains and climbed those hills within which took my life for a spin. Only could it be; at this place I found peace and God gave my mother back to me. And she became that which I needed to continue on and press my way through these moments of being open yet confused. Guess what she already knew and she stood by my side as I carried my child. Along with God holding my hand and feeding my child with his master plan as she grew in a dark land full of light from Heaven.

Could I be or is this a dream that I will soon wake from and be without child growing inside me.

I am what I am and man didn't understand! I let go of the streets to make things safe for my baby. It wasn't for me because I was self destructive and I could only see as far as my eyes showed me.

Now eighteen and time seems to keep moving in school trying to get through this change and keeping up with the name I made in the streets. But I was captivated by my baby's heart beat. Finding out who my real friends were left me with a lot of scares, yet I gained a place where I could see, maybe I found a new world to invest in me. In this place of peace and mysteries as my baby grows inside me. Tick tock time kept on ticking and my stomach got bigger. Now, my mother and I were closer than we ever been, even with that man still around (you know, the one with the iron fist). He was even trying to be a helper in this endeavor. He was the one who kept her from being close to her children who needed her the most. Now instead of hearing her being abused I saw her out of the room.

He and she helped me through, down to the last moment or two when she fell to her knees crying out "God please"!

A problem came forth my baby wouldn't come after two days of pain and fever I was done. "An emergency surgery will have to do, in order for you to pull through" said the doctor in the room. But God heard my mother's cry and there she was, my baby looking up high. As I looked at my master's gift he sent to me come alive it brought tears to my eyes. On that day, God gave her to me to start my new journey. In her was power from the pain as she turned over to look at me. The nurses could not believe what their eyes had seen while cleaning my baby.

Could I be what I am a mother in a foreign land yet ready to become the light for my shining star, my angel, and my first born the one who brought cover in the mist of a storm? Even though I didn't know the reason why God brought heaven to me from the sky I realized He had put me as a door keeper to an awesome soul. But I knew at that moment when I felt life come from me that my heart came alive and stepped out of misery. At that time I proclaimed I would be the best mother in Jesus name!

(DID I BECOME WHAT I WAS TO BECOME)

Do you know I spent many years looking at my mother be a mother I spent many days seeing her be under cover hiding her eyes from the pain and abuse and from the alcohol use. I knew that life was not for me or for my baby. Living in a home unstable either drags you in or saves you!

So I figured out what I did not want to be and became the best at what I wanted my child to see. Even though my world was a part of the streets I know I could give her the love that hid deep down inside of me. I was mother first then money followed very close. I wanted my child to have everything under and above the sun I guess like my daddy wanted for me. So I became a self made Queen.

I wanted to catch every tear she cried before they even fell from her eyes. I didn't want her heart to feel any pain nor her life to become a part of hell. I also realized you can only give to a life what you are willing to give up for that life and I was not ready to give up the streets so I became a woman of many colors. I was mother by day but when the arrow glass turn at night I became a woman of the streets, all over again. I had to claim my fame so I can have all that was offered in the game. Little did I know life was about to become a lesson of truth. Material things meant a lot to me in my world of captivity. The freshest of the freshest the smoothest of the smooth often called "Diva", so my ego grew. Never under estimated yet misunderstood from the eyes from the outside looking in, pretending they knew who I was. To them I was who they thought I was even in the darkness of this world.

Did I become what I was to become? Or did I become smarter to the facts of the streets that kept me from getting beat? I vowed that a man would never beat me or he would find himself in defeat crawling to his knees. That promise stayed with me but instead I lashed out from more grief.

No father around at this time for my child so I became the mother of many styles playing this game called life I would not give up without a fight. Many big names, many in the game were around me building me higher in the streets. My eyes could never tell the things I saw but my heart built up a stronger iron wall. I only let it down for my daughter to see the love I had hidden inside of me. Even though I let the world bury it beneath I kept a little for her to see.

Beneath the rebel of catastrophe is where the world could see the real me even when I hid, even when the streets couldn't find me I had the power to reach within and hold on to just a little piece of the God that was left holding on for dear life in me. I needed something to keep me sane so I can continue in the streets.

Am I who I am apart from darkness or did I allow darkness to consume me? Because I knew who I was suppose to be when God predestined me before my eyes could see. I believe before I was born I had a meeting with a great man and he said "I have you as a part of my master plan. I will give to you a body and allow you to be free as you walk the earth for me." So he molded me and shaped me and equipped me for the world but what I didn't know was once I got to my destination I wouldn't be at my destiny. The world was waiting at my mothers gates for me to show my face but if I only knew what the world had in store for me I would have held on to the gates of heaven and cried out God please help me. Once the world had a taste of who I was and in whom I came from it had a master plan of it's own to destroy me and take my throne. So I would not conquer the plan my master had but I would die in the rubble of this world where darkness stands.

*****People see what they want to see in you but the spirit in a person can see something no one else can see. The soul can see past your past, past your pain, past the iron wall and past your government name. The soul is the one part of you that even when all else fails, even with a lack of energy continues to climb from under hell an drag its self back to a place that connects him to the source that gives him power to over come. We are our worst enemy we knock our soul back down time after time. Our soul continues to thirst for the source and press toward it in order to survive the weight of the world. The soul has to stay connected to the power box which is God. All it takes is for the God in you to see the place of destiny even in the mist of pain and misery.

You see I didn't know what to believe. I allowed myself to take in the very things that were taking me down. I lost myself in my pain which caused my life to take a change. Be true to yourself! Always stay real being fake denies you true responses from God, the world and yourself. Release those things that keep you beneath your own catastrophe. Hold on to the one thing that feels right but your world tells you it's wrong.

Be the person looking from the outside in to yourself and don't be afraid to change the things that do not look right when you are looking in. Even in darkness you can find your way if you take your time and listen within. You will be guided by the power that never ends. To conquer your enemy you have to beat it at its own game. While your enemy speaks negative, you speak positive and feed yourself nothing but the best mentally, emotionally and physically until you over power that which held you beneath the rubble, pushed you into pain and caused you to be running in place, that's what I did.

Dig deep within and find that man or woman then start unloading all the rubble, all the pain, and all the misery to the one that says "cast your burdens upon me" which is the one that created you. Can you be emptied if you think you are too deep? Did you forget He already knows where you are? It sometimes seems as if the deeper you are the more He uses you for great assignments. Then you can truly know you are who you are even with the enemy out there to destroy, kill and steal.

DEAR GOD,

I CRY OUT TO YOU IN THE MIST OF THE PAIN.
I ALLOWED THE WORLD TO TAKE ME FROM MY PLACE. I KNOW YOU ARE WHO YOU ARE EVEN THOUGH I CAN'T HEAR YOUR VOICE OR SEE YOU, I STILL CRY OUT TO YOU. SAVE ME FROM MYSELF FOR I HAVE NO OTHER HELP. LORD I AM BURIED DEEP BENEATH THE PAIN AND MISERY OF THE STREETS AND NO ONE SEEMS TO BELIEVE IN ME. I CAST THIS DARKNESS ON THE CHRIST WITHIN AND I GO FREE TO WALK THIS EARTH FOR YOU AND CARRY OUT WHAT YOU HAVE FOR ME TO DO. MANY MISTAKES I HAVE MADE BUT YOU SAID THAT CAN BE ERASED IF I REPENT AND LET IT GO YOU WILL OPEN NEW DOORS. HERE I AM LOST IN A WORLD WITH MAN. ASHES TO ASHES AND DUST TO DUST I CAME; NOW I COME CALLING YOUR NAME! SOMETHING HAS TAKEN HOLD OF ME AND I CAN'T SEEM TO SHAKE IT FROM ME BUT I KNOW IF I JUST GET UP ENOUGH STRENGTH YOU WILL SAVE MY INNER MAN. I AM SORRY I STEPPED OUT OF YOUR WILL FOR ME AND INTO A WORLD OF MATERIAL THINGS. I NEED YOU TO EMPTY ME BECAUSE LIFE FEELS SO HEAVY. I AM TRYING TO DO IT ON MY OWN BUT I FOUND OUT THERE IS A MISSING PIECE THAT I NEED CONNECTED TO ME. LORD HERE I AM THE ONE YOU MADE A PART OF YOUR MASTER PLAN. I AM HERE UPON MY KNEES LOOKING AT ALL THE DIRT THE WORLD THREW AT ME AND I CAN'T SEEM TO FIND MY WAY TO THE PATH WHERE I CAN SEE YOUR FACE. SO GUIDE ME AND SEE ME THROUGH AS I TAKE THIS JOURNEY TO FIND YOU AGAIN. THANK YOU LORD FOR HEARING ME SO I CAN GET TO THE NEXT STAGE OF FINDING MY INNER BEING.

> THANKS, YOURS TRULY
> GAN'S INNER MAN

*** TRAVELING BACK IN TIME TRYING TO GET BACK FROM THE DARKNESS TO FIND THE FIRST DAY OF LIGHT IN MY DARKEST MOMENTS AS A CHILD!

I was lost in between many worlds. My eyes had seen so many things. It was kind of hard to fight through the debris. I remember being dropped off at my daddy's mom house (my grandmother) during the summers. Her house was full of many souls trapped between levels of death. They were lost in the medium of the after life, so I was told. People would think I was crazy because I would tell them my grandmother's house was haunted. She new it and she would always tell me "I don't need to be scared of the dead I need to fear the living, because the dead can't harm me unless I let it in." As I got older I didn't want to go to her house anymore, I use to because my daddy was there and that was the only time I could see him after he and my mom were no more. I believe those spirits got in him and his sister, because something went wrong with their minds. I don't know how true that is but my daddy use to say to me that I was playing around his head when I wasn't. My aunt jumped at me with a knife trying to kill me then she tried to set my grandmother's house on fire with me in it. She said an alien had taken over my body and I had to die so the real me could come back. That confused me even more in the mist of my life's pain and misery.

I used to wonder how much this little girl could take, before she cracked. When you're being passed around from place to place you begin to drown in who you are. The fight back to light becomes a maze because you are trying to figure out which way to go in the mist of the dead ends of other people's issues.

Did I become who I was to become! First I have to empty all the mess that I passed as I traveled through my mind of confusion. To find out who I am I have to break through the web that has entangled my mind. Hold on, you are on the road of finding someone you never thought would come into existence! We all travel roads unknown and do things we are not proud of but what we don't understand is we are who we are even apart from our darkness! And if you are going to walk through hell you might as well come out with something worth dying for! Jesus descended to the lower parts of the earth and took the keys that open up everything. Get your keys and find out who you are in the light! Step into the first day of the rest of your tomorrows.   **GENESIS 1 VS 5: GOD CALLED THE LIGHT DAY, AND THE DARKNESS HE CALLED NIGHT. SO THE EVENING AND THE MORNING WERE THE FIRST DAY.**

CHAPTER TWO

EMPTYING ME OUT FROM THE WORLD (E-H)

"IF WE STOP AND ALLOW GOD TO INCREASE HIMSELF IN US AND DECREASE US IN OURSELVES WE WILL FIND OUR TRUE SELVES."

EMPTY

Empty me from the anguish I feel! Spill me out from the mountains and hills bring me from the valleys below so that I can go the path I must go. Become the tube that sucks me dry and wipe the tears from my eyes as it empties me and release all the pain and misery I saw in the streets.

Become my Alpha and Omega so that I can become greater, while the world in me feels the anguish my soul has seen in the mist of you empting those things I allowed the world to pour in me.

Many tears I have cried at night upon these knees you gave to me. I continued to climb even in my sleep, the hard aches of the streets. It became known as I pushed to grow that the streets would try and take me down when I try to leave its grounds.

My soul is crying out it is losing the fight and the world is counting till lights out! I gasp for air as I'm being taken over through the death of my soul that this world has chosen. I was trying to keep my head above water, trying to hold on to some type of order yet I can't see what the next corner has for me. The enemy was standing at the door trying to keep me with many tricks up his sleeves.

Here I am walking on this earth but in my own paths lost in the middle of no where trying to get back to what I felt before the world grabbed hold of me. I was tightly caught up in chains bound with shackles of pain standing on a rope made of tears balanced by another man fears. Grabbing hold of what ever I saw near me leaving my mind unclear so I could not see that the enemy was truly after me. I didn't know that the place where they stood was held up by that man who was trying to get closer to hell; but he missed some steps on his way there. But what he didn't know is I held something inside of me that held the ability to see!

Then I did what the enemy did peeped into my own future in my head. I saw what God had for me if I just believed that I am who I am even in a dark land! I am who I am by whom I came from and no man can take me under. So I cried out with all that I was about and said "God please empty me out from what has taken me hostage and put me in captivity."

EMPTY!
Empty all that you did not place in me.
Empty the pain my eyes have seen.
Empty the things from that man; you know the one in the other room who brought the scares and wounds.
Empty the thing that made me who I am as I walked this land.
Empty the things that took away the little girl in me.
Empty the place where I couldn't be that little girl anymore. That little girl that yearned for a hug before her innocence was taken and torn from her.
Empty the hunger my belly felt when I was left without food. Empty the place where that man locked us in the house and took away the key so I couldn't run for help and no one could see.
Empty the scares and bruises within that stabs my inner man.
Empty the noises that live between my minds, which began the iron wall on the inside.
Empty the place where I looked out the window and saw my mother being dragged across the pavement screaming and hoping God would save her.
Empty the place where I heard my mother get beat.
Please empty the place where I could not sleep from the noise that disturbed my peace.
Empty the place where my eyes would not close until silence took over.
Empty the place where this man made me cleanse him and wash his feet.
Empty the place where he made me be a slave when my mother was away.
Empty, just empty that place!
The place where I no longer heard the birds sing, the place where my soul no longer danced to your melody!

The place where I did not smile anymore when my heart walked out the door; the place where I could not save my sister and me, the place my mother was scared to leave.

The place where my world had no more meaning, the place where I no longer believed I could be the very thing I strived to become when I was innocent and young. Empty that place where I was no longer daddy's little girl. Just empty me, empty me from that world.

Just empty all the pain and cover me from the rain.

Just empty the thing in me that keeps me from being free.

Just empty the place where I could no longer love where God frowned upon me yet showered his love.

Just empty the rubbish from the heart breaks, the dust from the heart aches, and the things that took my heart away.

Just empty the things that blinded me from seeing you in my dreams and buried the knowledge of you away from me.

Lord, empty me from whatever is holding me up on the cross because you already gave up your life for me. I need to get back to the place you said I am free; the place where your blood poured over me and erased all my sins away to prepare me for brighter days.

(FORGIVE AND FORGET)

For I had realized if I continued to hold on to my past I wouldn't reach my future. My past made me an iron wall in a world where I stood tall. I was holding on to my pain so I would not be stepped on and drug around by man in this world of captivity; upon this dark land.

For those shackles made of pain and those chains made of tears built me strong so I could not be broken with fear.

The things that made me are the very things that broke me even though I was broken down inside because of my past that was not going to last.

Those tears I cried were numbered to be my rope to the next level and fill me with hope for my tomorrows.

So I had to figure out what would make me better.

"Forgive" a voice said clearly for only your heart can see when you forgive then you can trust me."

For I forgive man (human, the world) for trying to destroy me because he did not know he was being used against me.

I forgive the world for not knowing my worth, for never looking past my pain and knowing my true inner man.

I forgive the world for not believing in me, for it allowed me to see I gave you power over me and as long as I held on to the pain I was your slave, therefore I lost and you gained.

I allowed you to be my eyes no matter how much I cried.

I allowed you to take from me, my crown for life and the victory that would soon, show me to my destiny.

I allowed you to be the reason I got money and the way I got it even when I had a lot in my pockets. I allowed you to keep me captive in captivity because I was not ready to leave the streets.

I allowed you to rule my world because I wanted the finer things in life even if it meant dying inside.

A thousand deaths I died even when I stood alive because I could not see to forgive will release the inner me. In those deaths my world stood stronger as my soul went under. So I had to try to forgive! I have to give it a try what could I lose part of me had already died!

I forgive the man that climbed on me and took my place of peace.

I forgive the man that left me out there to be slaughtered by the streets.

I forgive the man that allowed me to hear my mother being beat and see the black eyes left behind as she hid under the sheets.

I forgive the man that only thought of himself when it came down to life or death.

I forgive the man that stole my dreams of being a lawyer and other things.

I forgive the one who did not know how to take care of me and let me raise myself in the streets.

I forgive the ones that never understood that my God makes no mistakes; that's why I'm still here today.

I forgive the ones that were the reason for me never being stable where I saw more elementary schools than I saw grades.

I forgive the ones that were lost and dragged me in a world of poverty that tossed me to the traps of the streets.

I forgive everyone that did not grab hold of me yet said it will be ok if you just believe. What was I to believe in without directions or understanding?

I forgive everyone that did not save me from the pain and misery when I was under thirteen.

I forgive those that did not reach out and see that I was only crying out for help.

I forgive my teachers for not taking the time to reach me when you had more time with me.

I forgive; I truly forgive everyone especially those that did not know how to help me grow.

I forgive those that broke my heart and stepped on it without another thought.

I forgive those that hurt me when I was in a place of defeat trying to escape the streets.

I forgive! I forgive! I forgive! Now this mess must end. But first I must forgive myself more than anything else.

I forgive myself for the wrong choices I made.

I forgive myself for allowing the world to affect me.

I forgive myself for trying to write my own path, for falling into temptation, and walking in the darkness.

I forgive myself for holding on to pain and allowing it to eat at me.

I forgive myself for not realizing that I am the creator of the right destiny, not my own destiny if I walk on this earth for God and not me.

I forgive myself for not holding on to the things I received when my grandmother had me in church.

I ask you to forgive me to, everyone I hurt, everyone I was mean to, everyone that might have felt the wrath from my pain; I ask you again to forgive me.

NOW I SPEAK AS PAUL SPOKE;

BRETHERN, I DO NOT COUNT MYSELF TO HAVE APPREHENDED; BUT ONE THING I DO KNOW FORGETTING THOSE THINGS WHICH ARE BEHIND AND PRESSING FORWARD TO THOSE THINGS WHICH ARE AHEAD. I PRESS TOWARD THE GOAL FOR THE PRIZE OF THE UPWARD CALL OF GOD IN CHRIST JESUS. (PHILIPPIANS 3:13, 14)

Forgetting, I ask myself "how can you forget the very thing that forgot you." That forgot to help you grow, forgot to take time to let you know. That forgot you existed in this world of bondage trapped trying to break free from the robbers and thieves. Those that forgot to hold on to your innocence as a child, which took away that heavenly smile.

Those that forgot to wipe away your tears in the mist of your fears.

That forgot to say "I love you" when you needed them to.

That forgot to give a hug or two when life had your mind lost and confused.

That forgot you in the mist of their schedule of them trying to ride out the weather of their, own storm.

That forgot the world was waiting to pull you into their arms to fill darkness in your mind and keep your eyes blinded.

That forgot their purpose in life which knocked you down and stole your rights.

Forgetting, I ask myself "how can you forget the pain that held residence for so long?"

That caused your heart to sing to the emotions of pain as it ran from the storm and rain.

Forget those things that are behind us, after they have raced to a place to destroy the very soul that is trapped within the iron walls. Forget where I left pieces of my soul roaming in another man's inner man unattended. Forget that I was captured by someone pretending to be what I needed. I must forget!

I have to now capture my own soul from the other man and snatch it back in order for me to begin a journey that leaves what's behind me behind. I want to press my way to the prize! So I have to forget those which did not help me when I was trapped alive in the mist of those iron walls trying to catch my breath in between my falls. I realized if I can forget those things behind that took me from my path and shattered my dreams, which put me in bondage and tried to destroy me. If I can forget the chains of pain and shackles of tears then I can walk with no fear.

If I can forget the life after my birth and rebirth the life before my birth then I will stand in a place where my strength came from so I can continue to press forward and move on. Then I realized what's behind me is what blinded my eyes. So I closed them and forgot! I forgot that I was being deceived and took a moment to believe. I forgive you and me! Now, God can I see you? Now can I hear from you?

(GOD WHERE ARE YOU)

GOD where are you!
I looked out of my window wondering could He be close with all the noise and misery I couldn't find Him near me so the stars became my friends as I counted them to pretend that the hell I heard from the other room didn't exist in between those iron walls.

I wondered when happiness was given out was I missed. Many tears I dropped trying to figure out how to dismiss pain at the age of thirteen. Normal to our mind is what we see in sight and confusion is what life was like. In me I was fighting to keep my sanity while I cried out to God please hear me. For the noise had invaded my peace and my soul, for I couldn't hold my ears anymore.

How can the sound of a fist mixed with the screaming and abuse damage that inner child that's trying to get through?

I asked that I be saved but I can't see your face nor hear your voice from that loud noise within the walls of my mind. So I used my tears as the light that shines thinking you would find me through the night as I laid in my room looking up at you by my heavenly night light. Seeing those stars so bright; I couldn't understand why I couldn't hear from you! Yet I saw Angels coming through to rock me to sleep after hearing my mother get beat!

Waking up to a new day praying my mother will awake so I peeked into the other room just to see if she would move. Another day, another fight God saved us another night. The house seem calm from the noise but the walls are crying out from that fist that hit it in the mouth. New holes I counted in the wall as I measured the one growing inside me building up from the last catastrophe.

So I asked "where is He!"

Is He feeling this pain or is He holding it in his hand. Is He hearing my voice or is it lost in the noise. Is He, is He, Is He still In me or is it to much pain for Him to be!

I found a place buried deep within that held on to the God in me and I tried to visit there every now and then after all the noise had ended; from that room.

Some how I will find my way back through the debris that collapsed upon me when the world locked me in chains and left the key with the enemy! Not that I wanted to stay in captivity because if I could have found my way back to the God in me, in the mist of the noise going on in the walls of my mind I would have. But some way, some how I could not find my way back. So I learned how to survive in these worldly attacks.

God where are you, I am left here lost and confused looking for a way to escape the things that have taken me away. You said you would never leave me nor forsake me yet I stand in a world of misery. You said no weapon formed against me shall prosper yet the enemy has taken me captive.

You said ask and you shall receive, seek and you shall find, knock and the door shall be opened yet I have done all those things and nothing has opened up for me. I asked for peace and I received misery; I sought your face and the enemy gave me pain to erase it; I knocked on Heaven's doors in my mind yet it would not open and I still held on to the words you have spoken.

"You are the source of my supply; you wipe every tear from my eyes, if I can get enough strength to call your name I will be at a place to be saved." God you are the fight in me even when I was blind and could not see, you became the voice of reason in between my most difficult seasons.

God you are the power beneath my feet that allows me to stand strong in the mist of the heat. So God where are you? I am here on my knees, will you please rescue me? I'm calling for you to please save me before the enemy completely over takes me. I feel that you have stood back when I needed you the most and I can't understand how to get back close. Lord can you please allow me to understand something about this plan.

I know I have tried things out of pain but I need more shelter from this rain. Lord, can I? Can I please hear from thee! I need your mercy to come upon me. Lord I need to breath! Please speak to me!

(HOW LONG WILL YOU NOT HAVE MERCY ON ME?)

How do I get an answer from you? What in the world should I do? I seek to see your face or hear the voice that loves me anyway, but my heart feels erased from you. I can't hear you! Lord what do I do? Please have mercy on me I know I fell to the streets!

ZECHARIAH 1 VS 12: THEN THE ANGEL OF THE LORD ANSWERED AND SAID, "O LORD OF HOSTS, HOW LONG WILL YOU NOT HAVE MERCY ON JERUSALEM AND ON THE CITIES OF JUDAH, AGAINST WHICH YOU WERE ANGRY THESE SEVENTY YEARS?"

I didn't understand why God anger was with me when I was yet a child of captivity. My mind had been invaded by the noises of the world and my thoughts have landed me on the streets of hell! I was lost in a world of pain trying to escape the life that I obtained in my world of pain. Now I'm in the middle of no where and I don't know how to get back there.

I am looking for a place where I could be free a place where I can find me. I have done things my soul hid from and people have taken my heart and ran. I became street thinking it would comfort the emptiness within me. Instead my eyes saw things that devoured parts of my soul and transformed my spirit from hot to cold. Then I gave my body to those who didn't deserve to walk away with a piece of my soul. So here I am half of woman deprived of all of me because the other half was in captivity. I gave it to the streets and my flesh rose up and beat my spirit down so that the enemy could take over these grounds.

A thousand deaths my soul died fighting to stay alive but my flesh won in the mist of another man's storm. My mother said I turned into the exodus at sixteen. Just maybe something took over me! Something the world put in me to break me down so that I wouldn't have the strength to get back up. Then my mind would be stuck, in a battle that is not mine so I began to fight it blind. I guess I had lost my mind and the enemy knew all about me. He kept my mind occupied with the streets; by giving me things of the world that caught my eyes and kept my flesh alive. How can I still trust you when my inner man is all abused? I guess because that's all I felt I knew!

I felt the pain trample down my inner skin causing bruises within. My heart bleeds on the inside from the deaths of my soul, and I'm running in and out of dark holes. How! How can I, I am calling while my soul is dying. I asked to be saved and the pain has escaladed to another level. Now I can't determine which way is heaven. I cry out to you from the flame that burns within screaming and asking for the water that cools my skin.

I am hiding within my walls feeling my soul fumble and crawl. My soul was trying to escape the weight that had pressed down upon it but it had no strength to stand. It was going under until it fumbled around for God's unchanging hand. God you said you will never leave me nor forsake me; where are you? Why can't I see? How do I get back to thee? My soul scrambled for some words and a soft voice was heard.

<u>**THIS IS WHAT GOD SPOKE TO ME FROM WITHIN MY IRON WALLS:**</u>
"THOUGH YOU ARE IN PAIN AND MISERY YOUR WALK HAS BEEN ORDERED BY ME. PAIN COMES TO MAKE YOU STRONG SO THAT IN DUE TIME YOU WILL BECOME THE PERSON WHO BROKE FREE AND CAN STAND FOR ME. I AM BUILDING YOU TO BE SOLID AS A ROCK. I KNOW YOU HAVE BEEN TRAMPLED OVER AND STEPPED ON I WAS STILL COVERING YOU IN THE MIST OF THOSE STORMS. I KNOW THAT YOU DON'T UNDERSTAND WHY I ALLOWED YOU TO WALK IN MISERY BUT IN DUE TIME YOU WILL SEE. YOUR PAIN WILL BRING FORTH YOUR DESTINY AS YOU WALK OUT OF CAPTIVITY. YOUR LIFE HAS BEEN FILLED WITH MY MERCY YOU JUST COULDN'T DETERMINE IF YOU WERE WORTH IT. I COVERED YOU ALL THE YEARS THAT YOU ROAMED THE STREETS AND DIDN'T HEAR OR SEE ME. I WAS YOUR EYES WHEN YOU COULD NOT SEE. WHY DO YOU THINK YOU HAVE ESCAPED TROUBLE WHEN IT WAS RIGHT AT YOUR FEET? WHY DO YOU THINK YOU WERE NEVER CAUGHT? I HAD ANOTHER PLAN THAT MAN KNEW NOTHING ABOUT. SO MY CHILD DON'T YOU WEEP I WILL PUT YOUR ENEMY BENEATH YOUR FEET! YOU MUST UNDERSTAND JUST BECAUSE YOU DON'T HEAR FROM ME, DOES NOT MEAN YOU ARE NOT WHERE I NEED YOU TO BE. FOR YOUR DESTINY WILL SHOW YOU, WHY SO MUCH PAIN." So I said "Lord I know your mercy is something I don't deserve for some reason my life have been cursed. Can you break this curse from me so that I can step into my true destiny? I want it to end hear so my child will not transact this curse and keep it going another generation. Lord I know sufficient is your grace that has saved me while I was yet in sin scrambling with the enemy."

I was doomed at birth when hell heard me cry because God's word was coming alive. satan took vengeance because he didn't want me to survive. he was thinking of a master plan that will cause my life to transition into another state of mind. he went for the weakest link, which was my father, so it caused my mother and father to sink. When they jumped ship he jumped in and began to disturb my inner man. he began to hinder me and speak things of deceit. he tried to put in my mind to take my own life, he told me

God has seen the things I have done and he will never forgive me, and I was dead at his feet.

This darkness has clouded around me yet something on the inside is trying to get free. I realized that even in the darkness, my soul held a light and though it may be buried, it was not giving up without a fight. Even when I didn't feel God's mercy was upon me it had to have been because I lived a life where things weren't always safe; I walked the streets that consumed my spiritual space. I was at a place of no return; the iron wall could no longer move to its own beat. It had walked right into another wall that would not allow me to move forward without my true source. So, I continued the fight even when the enemy said run and give up your life.

PSALM 144 VS 1-8: BLESSED BE THE LORD MY ROCK, WHO TRAINS MY HANDS FOR WAR, AND MY FINGERS FOR BATTLE- MY LOVING KINDNESS AND MY FORTRESS, MY HIGH TOWER AND MY DELIVERER, MY SHEILD AND THE ONE IN WHOM I TAKE REFUGE, WHO SUBDUES MY PEOPLE UNDER ME. LORD, WHAT IS MAN THAT YOU TAKE KNOWLEDGE OF HIM? OR THE SON OF MAN, THAT YOU ARE MINDFUL OF HIM? MAN IS LIKE A BREATH; HIS DAYS ARE LIKE A PASSING SHADOW. BOW DOWN YOUR HEAVENS, O LORD, AND COME DOWN; TOUCH THE MOUNTAINS, AND THEY SHALL SMOKE. FLASH FORTH LIGHTNING AND SCATTER THEM; SHOOT OUT YOUR ARROWS AND DESTROY THEM. STRETCH OUT YOUR HAND FROM ABOVE; RESCUE ME AND DELIVER ME OUT OF GREAT WATERS, FROM THE HAND OF FOREIGNERS, WHOSE MOUTH SPEAKS LING WORDS, AND WHOSE RIGHT HAND IS A RIGHT HAND OF FALSEHOOD.

I never knew that God was preparing me for the fight of my life and the fight for my life. The world may frown upon those that are living the street life, or from the projects and those that were left with nothing after tragedies, but God prepares us for greatness. Just by looking, you can never tell what a person has been through! So why frown! Why not ask? The fight for their life may be happening! And God may have sent you to save them.

If someone does not reach out to someone in pain or even see their pain, then they can not judge or talk down on anyone. There are things in life during our struggles that causes us to make decisions based on our mind frame. I know a lot of people would never understand my walk, or other people walks that have been through their own pain and struggles. But, I was always told "LEAN NOT ONTO YOUR OWN UNDERSTANDING BUT IN ALL YOUR WAYS ACKNOWLEDGE HIM AND HE WILL DIRECT YOUR PATH." (PROVERBS 3 VS 5-6) If you have never been there then you can not understand nor judge. Just know God gave all of us our own walk and purpose and if we fall that does not mean we can't get up. Don't allow your blinders to cause you to fall for the enemy tricks. We all fall short! We are all moments from being in a place of judgment or defeat.

One day the people of this world will realize that everyone does not have the same mentality as others. They will realize we are all individuals and though we may come from different environments we are very similar underneath. It is our circumstances and places in life that makes our struggles and the outcome of our situations different. We all serve a purpose we just serve them at different times in the universe. Some people are ahead of others because of their ancestors, their social life at birth and their place in the circle of life. Also because their minds may have been feed what is needed from birth to develop strength for life. But they are not better than others for God's mercy is upon us all.

I realized that God's mercy had been upon me even as I subjected myself to the streets. I just was too blind to see and by that time I had been cast down within, fighting against the wind, trying to understand how my flesh became the man. Though man thought I was cast down, God had it all figured out; my walk was a part of my purpose. Destiny was crawling toward me.

CHAPTER THREE

I AM CAST DOWN YET UNCONQUERED (I TO L)

THOUGH I HAVE BEEN LABELED A STATISTIC I CAN NOT BOW DOWN, I HAVE TO RISE TO REACH MY DIVINE GROUNDS.

(I WANT GIVE UP; SOMETHING IN ME IS FIGHTING TO BE SET FREE!)

I felt the world had given up on me after it through me to the dogs and gave me a deadly way to see my way standing in the enemies grave. I had been fighting for my sanity, I had been fighting my inner being and my inner being was fighting for me. The child in me was crying out because it never had a chance to live it's time out. I had to bury my heart to survive the pain; I continued in a place that I felt was safe. I was running the streets making money without being guilty. I have been in places I should have never been, trying to come upon worldly riches. I was connected to the game that had my streets on lock, never blinked twice not even in a drought. I was lost in a world of sin; spinning in a circle of darkness something in me was trying to reach out because it would not give up even though lights was out. It was sitting in darkness trying to see how it could still help me to escape the streets!

I never lost a battle that came upon me as I scrambled in the streets. I wouldn't back down to anything that tried to bring me down. I was already living life on the enemy grounds so why not gain my worldly crown. I knew someone was praying for me because I never went under in the streets. Only my soul was perishing because I was getting deeper in the streets. I had an insight within. I felt trouble before it took flight. I stayed from under the radar of the men in black so I would not become hot on the streets.

From my worldly blood line and studying the people of the streets I mastered the game that helped me eat. But, I became tired of watching my back. My mind was running between two worlds that symbolized my struggles inside and out. I had been broken into pieces stripped of my dreams but I knew something was roaring inside me. I had been walking through fire and my soul was burned and darkness was upon me but I still had to learn how to see my way through, because I couldn't hear anyone. The words people spoke to me did not register.

Then, I realized that I was in the fire of life to be refined; God was making a precious piece of gold with diamonds all around it. Gold is put in fire and it is the fire that exalts its greatness and enhances its value. It is in the fire where I was being molded into the jewel that will soon shine for God. My outside may seem burned but when I come out of the furnace you will only be able to judge me from the inside. Next time you will not be able to see the burns of life because God has me now and though the heat may be up high the fire can't touch me. Read in the bible (**Daniels 3 vs. 19-30**). With trusting and having faith in God fire can't touch you, no matter how hot it gets.

MY SOUL SPEAKS: "I CAN NOT GIVE UP EVEN THOUGH MAN HAS CAST ME DOWN MY LIFE MAY LOOK LIKE DEFEAT BUT I AM STILL AROUND. I AM BREATHING OFF TOXIC WASTE THAT MAN POURED ON ME DAY BY DAY AS I WONDERED IN THOSE STREETS. UNDERNEATH ALL THE MESS SOMETHING STILL WOULD NOT GIVE ME A REST. IT FELT LIKE A SEED WAS BURIED DEEP DOWN IN THE EARTH SURFACE OF MY SPIRIT. IT WAS COVERED WITH DIRT AND IT WAS TRYING TO BUST ITS WAY OUT FROM THE DARKNESS AND DROUGHT OF NOT BEING CONNECTED TO THE WATER THAT FLOWED THROUGH (HOLY SPIRIT). YET, THAT SEED JUST WOULD NOT GIVE UP BECAUSE SOMETHING DOWN IN THAT DARK HOLE WAS GIVING IT LIFE TO STAY STRONG. YOU COULDN'T SEE IT, BUT IT'S THERE AND THE FIGHT TO LIVE WAS GOING NO WHERE. IT (I) WAS CAST DOWN UNDERNEATH THE GRAVEL AND DIRT YET UNCONQUERED BY THE WEIGHT OF THE EARTH. IN THE FIRE OF PAIN THERE WAS A HAND THAT GRABBED HOLD OF ME EVEN IN THE DARKNESS OF CAPTIVITY."

PSALM 139 CHP 10-12: EVEN THERE YOUR HAND SHALL LEAD ME, AND YOUR RIGHT HAND SHALL HOLD ME. IF I SAY, "SURLY THE DARKNESS SHALL FALL ON EVEN THE NIGHT SHALL BE LIGHT ABOUT ME; INDEED, THE DARKNESS SHALL NOT HIDE FROM YOU, BUT THE NIGHT SHINES AS THE DAY THE DARKNESS AND THE LIGHT ARE BOTH ALIKE TO YOU.

(JUDGE ME FROM THE INSIDE)

Just because I was in the streets did not mean I didn't continue to pray at night. It did not mean I had no mercy, because even in my walk I helped those that didn't have. I feed those that were hungry I gave to those that were in need. So, it didn't mean God and I did not walk in the same space at times. Jesus walked among thieves and killers. He changed their life and used them for His glory. I was told often by my grandmother "no sin is greater or lesser than the other, and that we have all sinned and fallen short of his glory." She used to tell me you were not going to church for nothing as a little girl; God did not put it in us to send you just because. Your time in church was for a reason; those words were planting a seed for your latter days. She knew I would one day soon find my way back to the King.

I always asked God to forgive me. I would feel he did. That's how I knew I wasn't all the way lost. That's how I knew that even though I was damaged with pain something in me had a special connection to the higher source. That's why I was saved so many times and kept some how. My mind would warn me or something inside gave alarm when things wasn't right. I had this gift even in darkness where I often saw things and dreamed things that would soon come to pass. I don't know why I was chosen with that gift but that would explain a lot of things later. That's why something in me was unconquered. It would not bow down and give up its spiritual crown with out a great fight going down.

My age was not a part of my growth. I felt I grew faster in my mind than I did in age. I believe I knew things grown people wished to have known or I thought I did anyway. I saw the world from a different sight and thought that was life. I grew up very quickly in my mind. I had an internal survival kit resting inside of me. An innocent mind is filled with grace until pain invades its space, then it kicks off a survival growth, like an adult.

I would never settle for just anything. I never understood why grown ups did. I looked at them and wondered how their mind works. If I knew something was wrong why they didn't. If I saw things behind closed doors why didn't they realize life was worth much more? Why did they not understand they were the fruits I needed to eat from to build my character and find what stood inside of me before the streets? I was lost in other people worlds and couldn't figure out my own.

Let me take you back a little so you will understand where some of my pain came from; After not having lights for what ever reason and moving from place to place I was tired. I was mad at my mom's boyfriend (the man with the iron fist) and I had so much anger built inside of me for him and any other man that was near me giving me grief. I know people can only do what they know. I know my mother was working hard. She would work from sun up to sun down to make sure the bills were paid. This man, he didn't care one way or another of the damage he had caused in our life. He was walking in his own tragedies and pain of his past and really didn't know it. So we became his victims, he was putting his pain on us. He had been through so much pain and really didn't understand life. He didn't even know he was damaged goods and that he was open for the enemy to use him to destroy the word God had spoken in us. He was just living life as he knew it and how he was. What you are is what you give out. He was lost, hurt, in pain and all about himself, so that's what he gave. He only wanted to control my mom and us. A man that has to control has low self esteem and issues unseen. So he gives to you his pain. **That's why it's important to know who you are and to acknowledge that something is wrong before you subject yourself to other people's lively hood.**

"I was only about fourteen contemplating a man's death. In my head either we had to go or him. I believe in his head it was us before him. He made life unbearable because he was unbearable to himself. He (the man with the iron fist) would often lie to my mother and she would believe him so it really didn't matter anymore. When she would leave to go to work he would make us do things that a child had no business doing for a man that is not her father. It was bad enough we had to cook for him (my sister and I).

He would make us rub his back while he was lying in the bed just waking up. He would make us shave him and clean his face. He would make us rub his feet and just things that made me feel nasty and uncomfortable as a little girl. I was already angry at him! One day my sister and I decided that we wanted him gone. This particular day there was some boric acid in the kitchen so we decided to pour it in his food. The container said it kills rats and the man with the iron fist was a big rat to us at that time. We sat by the door to see if anything would happen. He called for us to get the plate but all of it was gone. Nothing happened! Now I thank God because we really didn't understand death we just understood pain and he was the pain and we wanted him to go away.

    My sister was so funny, one day I had to do his hair and she had to shave him. My sister shaved all the hair off parts of his body. She shaved his eyebrows, his mustache, his beard, and hair on his fingers and toes. He hadn't realized it because he had fallen asleep. When my mother got home she looked at him and started laughing. She told him to look in the mirror he was so mad. That may have been the last time we had to work on him because shortly after that I started refusing to. All my playmates would be outside and we had to be in doing that crap. I got tired of him and I started having screaming matches with him. When my mom came home he would blame everything on me. I really didn't care anymore. He made sure she would believe him and not us. After that I vowed to make life a living hell for him as he had made for me.

    I began to never be at home. I was in the streets of hell; in and out of clubs trying to be seen as I walked into catastrophe. Where ever the crowd was live I stood there with a smile. My best friend and I used to call each other sisters. We were always together. She was a little of my sanity. Her mom didn't want us to be friends anymore. I was hurt because I was losing my best friend since 5th grade, because her mother didn't understand; I was just a child walking in pain. One thing I did know was how to survive in the streets. I was not going to let anything happen to her. I wasn't all the way damaged I just had a lot of freedom because of the things that was going on in my home.

I started getting into every sport at school just to escape my home life. I wanted to keep people from knowing about the lack and abuse. I was trying to stop the fighting in my mind. I was a beast inside! I put it toward sports. I tried not to let anyone beat me at anything, especially not boys. I was so competitive in school and the streets. I was living a double life, as a teenager! Something drove me! I refused to have given the world anything else to destroy me with so I tried to destroy what ever got in my way by beating them at their own games, both in school and in the streets.

I did not want to lose at anything because I felt life had already lost me. I never let anyone know what was going on in my house only people that saw it knew. I was trying to hide my pain because I didn't want them to ever find out that I lived in a house of hell. Kids are smarter than what people give them credit for. Kids have a way of covering things up. They have a way of juggling many worlds. They have away of nurturing their own pain by instinct at least I did before fifteen.

The world was very colorful to me as a child before all the pain festered inside. I felt as if there was nothing I couldn't accomplish. I felt the adults in my life looked at life as if it was black and white which caused a lot of worldly issues for us (the kids). My child's mind knew what she wanted and was not afraid to go get it. People say you need to often allow the child in you to emerge because the imagination of a child is powerful. I was always taught a child is meant to be seen and not heard. The bible says "out of the mouth of babes…" which one is it?

I didn't know, so I learned at an early age how to block people out and things out. The only thing I had not mastered was blocking the noise from the other room out and the visualization of my mother's bruised face. I felt all we had to do was leave and the noise would go away! If it was that easy! As a child I would see the impossible and guide myself to it. In my mind as a child there were no limits until someone proved me wrong or led me down the wrong paths. I saw adults guide and raise kids off of their emotions and what they felt out of lust.

One day I told my mother I loved her and she said she loved me too, so I asked her "if you love us why would you not leave that man." I went on to ask her why she allowed him to keep hurting her and us. I told her it hurts us when he hurts her. She told me that "I could not give to her what a man could and I could not love her the way a man could and that I am a child and I won't understand." She went on to say "when I get older I would understand." That was the first time I thought in my mind something was wrong with my mom. I knew she was drinking a lot at this time, but she was so smart. I wondered how she could make such a stupid statement. I told myself that day that I would never end up thinking like her when it came to a man. I would never settle for a man just not to be alone. I was very disturbed and hurt; I felt my mother was choosing a man over her children.

I really felt my mom was blind to the fact. I knew that things where not right and I acknowledged that. As a child I spoke what was on my mind and didn't realize it may have hurt, or didn't really care if it hurt. I just wanted someone to see the big picture as I saw it.

I believe a lot of parents are self centered and don't realize it. What they should realize is once they make a decision to have children or become parents, it's no longer about them! At least until God says they are done in the process of raising them. I am sorry to say that but it's true. I even had to realize that it was no longer about me, even when I was in the streets and walking in darkness. The most important role parents hold in their children lives is making sure that the children are raised with morals, values, and God's words. They need to make sure they are not teaching and raising themselves all the time. I know by experience it is not easy to work, raise, teach and instill all a child needs, but no one said it would be. **Proverbs 22 vs. 6: Train up a child in the way he should go, and when he is old he will not depart from it.

I have always loved my mother no matter what, she became my best friend. She used to always tell me she was my best friend when I was in the street and didn't want to hear her. She was one of the best cooks I knew.

She was very smart, beautiful, and so strong to me, I just did not understand why she kept herself in such an abusive unhealthy relationship. I begin to think she just did not know any better. I wondered why she did not rescue us if she did not want to rescue herself. Maybe she didn't know that what she was going through was killing us just as well as her self?

I just did not understand, until one day my sister and I heard my mother and him (the man with the iron fist) having a heated argument in their room! I don't know if they had been drinking this night or not, we thought they were going to fight so we were sitting by my mother's door to help her (we were a little older by now). He told my mother to get rid of us that he didn't want us with them. My mom was crying and she told him she couldn't because she was all we had. She went on to ask him "where would we go?" Some kind of way it came out that one of the main reason she had not left him was because he had threaten her saying if she left him he would kill us and her. That's a hard pill to swallow.

At that time I realized in a sense she had chosen us, even with him still there. She chose to take the beatings and shake it off in order to secure our lives. No matter what knocked my mom down she would get up and keep going. She used to always tell me when I was hurting and confused to never let anything keep me from going forward, that I could do what ever I put my mind to despite of everything. I thought; despite of living in a house with a man that didn't value your life or your children's life; despite of the generational curse on your life; despite of the hopelessness, the sleepless nights and the dark tunnels within, you have to get up and keep pressing forward.

So in my darkest moments I was still learning my most valuable lessons. Even with seeing her beaten I also saw her get up and keep going. I learned in life no matter what tries to take me down, no matter what hurt me, no matter how bad things may seem I had to get up and keep going. With that, I was taught not to fall for anything no matter what the circumstance might be. Even seeing her drunk I was learning I did not want to be a drinker. That alcohol did not make your problems go away it enhanced them.

I felt she only knew what she saw. Inside she was a jewel in the mist of debris and no one dusted her off to see her value, after darkness invaded her mind. She could always see the good and possibilities in everyone else but herself.

She made choices she thought were the best thing at that time with what she had and knew. She is my mother! <u>You only</u> get one! No matter what decisions she may have made that I thought were wrong she was and still is my mother. I loved her no matter what I just wanted her to succeed. Even if I didn't understand, God did and still does! And if he trusted her with my life then how can I question his mysteries.

While the enemy was trying to take me hostage my grandparents, my Uncle J and my aunts (on my mother side of the family) tried to help me be a little grounded, as a little girl. I felt because they knew what I was going through they tried to baby me a little and show me as much love as they could in the mist of their own life of struggles and trials.

We lived with my Uncle J and aunt m sometimes in the mist of our moves. He was very stern and would whip me! I just thought he was so hard and though I didn't understand it then, I thank him now for being that man in my life that truly loved me! He loved and cared enough to correct me when there was no other man to do so.

I guess in the mist of the pain God was still trying to leave some type of balance, even though my life was weighed down with pieces of hell there was a place I would often try to get to! My grandparents; I was my grandfather's Gan baby; I was my grandmother's baby and that's how they tried to treat me in the mist of the alcohol use and abuse. Now they could not save me because the streets had taken over me.

My early judgment!

I began to dress up my outside to escape my inner darkness. I thought the outer appearance was the most important appearance. I had been teased and talked about so much by kids in school. They talked about my cloths and my payless shoes; they talked about my hair and teased me about my name. I was already in pain because of the environment of my home. It wasn't enough! The kids became a constant reminder of my lack, of my issues, of my darkness, of going from riches to rags. Once I turned sixteen I made a decision to make my own money to get cloths, shoes and anything else I felt I wanted. If I was beautiful and put together on the outside then no one would ever tell what I was dealing with on the inside. They could not judge my situation because they would only see my outer appearance. They could never know I feared for my mother, my sisters and my life.

I could not let any one know that inside I felt so ugly and empty. My mother use to say "beauty is skin deep, that it does not matter how your hair looks, and what you have on". I did not agree with her, at all! I didn't think she understood and she didn't know what I was feeling on the inside that caused me to be that way. So I really didn't grab hold to that concept especially at that time. I had to be dressed from head to toe. I had my own diva status to up hold. I didn't like anything out of place and my time was precious and counted for everyday.

I had begun to no longer care about what people said or thought about me. I felt they didn't help me nor put cloths on my back, so what did they have to say to me. I had an, I don't care attitude! The way people acted toward me did not bother me anymore. My iron wall made me believe I was superior and in my world I was. No matter what people said they could not take that from me. I felt they had taken everything else that meant anything on the inside, so no matter what they weren't going to take my outer look. At this point, they surely could not touch the inner me that was posted behind the iron wall.

So if you see me please don't judge me from my outer view or my circumstances nor my environment just look in my eyes and pierce through my soul and see I am trying to pull and press my way through those dark holes to discover my true destiny.

Something in me was dying and was leaving me confused. I don't know how death begins on the inside but I know how life feels in the mist of those deaths; confusing! Something was killing me slowly! I was powerless! At least I thought I was! But it was my flesh that was losing power while my spirit was gaining strength. *****ROMANS 8 VS 36: AS IT IS WRITTEN: FOR YOUR SAKE WE ARE KILLED ALL DAY LONG, WE ARE ACCOUNTED AS SHEEP FOR THE SLAUGHTER**

(KNOWLEDGE IS POWER; WITH POWER COMES RESPONSIBILITIES)

Know that no knowledge is the same as walking around with the wrong type of knowledge. With it you gain destructive power. **PROVERBS 25 VS 28: WHOEVER HAS NO RULE OVER HIS OWN SPIRIT IS LIKE A CITY BROKEN DOWN, WITHOUT WALLS.** That destructive power causes you to make the wrong decisions. The wrong decisions will cause us to fall into a life of bondage, which causes us to become self destructive in our present state.

Everyone has something that imprisons their true being which imprisons the mind, which causes the spirit to become torn, which causes the soul to become bound by enemy chains. I had allowed pain to bind me. I became one of my worst enemies. I started seeing that I held my own freedom, yet I had imprisoned myself behind the iron walls of hell.

I allowed the things and issues from the world to pour in me. So I must have the power to set myself free. Free from the bondage that bounded me to the game. Knowledge from where I came. All this time I was the blame for allowing things to contaminate me. Yes words were thrown at me; people even tried to take me down but that didn't mean I had to give it power. Though my innocence was stolen and my life had yet unfolded, I still had the breath of life. I had stress till I could not breathe because I had the weight of legends pressing against me. Yet only I could choose what to believe. I held inside me the tool I needed to set me free, from my life's tragedies.

I roamed the streets thinking I could find a place that defined me. I could say I didn't know but I was given knowledge before my birth. I became my worst enemy, you see! I was the destruction of myself after hell pushed my life into deaths.

It is hard to live life without a guide line when you have been brought up in a harmful environment. Even though I grew up in the church from birth when hell stepped in I soon let all that go. You have to figure out what to hold on to and what to let go. The only thing wrong with that is as a child you soak up all this negative energy and you don't understand how to release it. So you keep it in until an explosion takes place. That explosion kills something in you that connected you to the source. Then it affects everything around you, especially your mind. Once that connection is gone, once that death takes place; the world no longer looks pretty. The blinders go up and you feel everyone is against you. Instead of spiritual power you gain power in the flesh.

It feels like its wrong but it doesn't register as wrong in the mind. So the knowledge you are gaining is knowledge of how to manipulate the spiritual realm to rise in the worldly realm. As you rise on the worldly realm your soul encounters deaths after deaths. Death has taken control and your soul begins to lose.

Where does the responsibility lie now? How do you remove blinders from your eyes without knowledge to keep you alive?

Though I felt God hands had been taken from me and he had his back turned towards me I knew it was for a reason. He did not want to see the destruction I was putting my soul through. Though my soul was not giving up it was in torment. It held on to the knowledge that God gave it freely before birth. Buried down in the rebels of life it held on to a little light. Even after many deaths my soul held on to something down there! It held on to something that held the power to set it free from pain and misery.

HEBREW 2 VS 14: IN ASMUCH THEN AS THE CHILDREN HAVE PARTAKEN OF FLESH AND BLOOD, HE HIMSELF LIKEWISE SHARED IN THE SAME, THAT THROUGH DEATH HE MIGHT DESTROY HIM WHO HAD THE POWER OF DEATH, THAT IS, THE devil.

In us flows blood, it keeps us alive with much power. God gave it, its job in man to speak to every vessel in the body to work together with the breath of God to keep life going. By its name, the blood had inherited the responsibility of bringing the enemy down. Since satan's responsibility is to bring death to you. You have the responsibility to yourself to bring forth life to your soul; knowledge is power. You have to dig deep down within and bring forth everything God put in you despite of what has been cast down upon you.

There is a big word that we must fight for and that is will power which comes from the very word that God spoke over your life. Without will power we waiver, we give up our strength to something we feel has more power over us. When we do that it causes something in us to feel destroyed and torn down. That's why gaining knowledge allows you to gain power over that which has cast you down or given up on you. There is power in you to keep going no matter how you feel on the inside, no matter what covers your inner man; the word continues to help you stand.

JOHN 1 VS 1: IN THE BEGINNING WAS THE WORD AND THE WORD WAS WITH GOD, AND THE WORD WAS GOD. The enemy was after the word! It was God's word that spoke life in me and created my destiny. It was not about me it was about me finding the knowledge that will allow me to hear the word, receive it and act on it. ***ISAIAH 11 VS 9: THEY SHALL NOT HURT NOR DESTROY IN ALL MY HOLY MOUNTAIN, FOR THE EARTH SHALL BE FULL OF THE KNOWLEDGE OF THE LORD AS THE WATERS COVER THE SEA.** For God had given me knowledge freely but I chose to use it for the wrong things, so I ended up giving the enemy power to proceed with his attack to snatch from me the things God spoke over my life.

"Oh lord, I am sorry, please renders it back to me so that my soul will find its way back to see beyond what I allowed the world to pour in me."

~~KNOWLEDGE ONE ON ONE~~

*PROVERBS 19 VS 2: ALSO IT IS NOT GOOD FOR A SOUL TO BE WITHOUT KNOWLEDGE, AND HE SINS WHO HASTENS WITH HIS FEET.

**ECCLESIASTES 7 VS 12: FOR WISDOM IS A DEFENSE AS MONEY IS A DEFENSE, BUT THE EXCELLENCE OF KNOWLEDGE IS THAT WISDOM GIVES LIFE TO THOSE WHO HAVE IT.

***ECCLESIASTES 9 VS 10: WHATEVER YOUR HAND FINDS TO DO, DO IT WITH YOUR MIGHT; FOR THERE IS NO WORK OR DEVICE OR KNOWLEDGE OR WISDOM IN THE GRAVE WHERE YOU ARE GOING.

****HOSEA 4 VS 6: MY PEOPLE ARE DESTROYED FOR LACK OF KNOWLEDGE. BECAUSE YOU HAVE REJECTED KNOWLEDGE, I ALSO WILL REJECT YOU FROM BEING PRIEST FOR ME; BECAUSE YOU HAVE FORGOTTEN THE LAW OF YOUR GOD, I ALSO WILL FORGET YOUR CHILDREN.

******HOSEA 6 VS 1-3: COME, AND LET US RETURN TO THE LORD; FOR HE HAS TORN, BUT HE WILL HEAL US; HE HAS STRICKEN, BUT HE WILL BIND US UP. AFTER TWO DAYS HE WILL REVIVE US; ON THE THIRD DAY HE WILL RAISE US UP, THAT WE MAY LIVE IN HIS SIGHT. LET US PURSUE THE KNOWLEDGE OF THE LORD. HIS GOING FORTH IS ESTABLISHED AS THE MORNING; HE WILL COME TO US LIKE THE RAIN, LIKE THE LATTER AND FORMER RAIN TO THE EARTH.

THIS BECAME ONE OF MY FAVORITE SCRIPTURES:
*****ECCLESIASTES 9 VS 11: I RETURNED AND SAW UNDER THE SUN THAT- THE RACE IS NOT TO THE SWIFT, NOR THE BATTLE TO THE STRONG, NOR BREAD TO THE WISE, NOR RICHES TO MEN OF UNDERSTANDING, NOR FAVOR TO MEN OF SKILL; BUT TIME AND CHANCE HAPPEN TO THEM ALL.

MY SOUL CRIES OUT

My soul cries;

I stand with only my words to self; I shall bring forth life from this death.

I shall become the success in tragedy because I will stand from my knees before He uncovers who I am in Him.

For I shall walk on the shore of knowledge and bring back wisdom so that I can understand that my life is with Him and not man.

Because, who am I without Him other than the sand that blows into the sea, lost and confused without eyes to see, gasping for the breath in which He blew in me.

Now I hold on to what ever is near me and take my last breath as the world believes and allow my soul to breathe the breath of destiny.

My soul cries out to thee. I shall uncover the knowledge and see beyond what the world allowed me to believe.

I stand from my knees and walk from that place called misery and step into a life of unlimited possibilities.

My soul cries out tears of not knowing and God wipes them away with His clouds of knowledge;

My soul cries out tears of pain and God wipes them with His hands of understanding;

My soul cries out tears of fear and my God brushes them away with His wings giving me the wisdom to see there are no limits for me! My soul is all cried out!

(LEADING ME TO THE SHADOWS OF DEATH)

Leave me alone, I feel my soul is transitioning inside. It was pushing me from street life head on into this game called real life.

I wanted things to be different for my kids. My oldest daughter was already being labeled the first trap baby in our hood. Right in front of our house she had already been in the center of a drive by shooting; bullets were coming down from off the top of a hill. That could have been deadly because bullets have no eyes and no name on them.

My baby was not going to be like me. I was not going to let her or me fall into the curse that seemed to rest over my family. I did not want her to be in the streets or in the mist of the game. From my worldly blood line I became that which took hold of my father and his father. The curse would stop here even if I had to stay on my knees.

I never carried myself as a hustler around certain people even though they looked at my outer appearance and judged me, as that. Only those that were my street brothers and those close to me knew.
From the outside I looked like a girl who had a man with a lot of money, from the inside I was making my own money. I was too independent to wait on a man. My outer appearance was very important to me; I did not want anyone to see my pain so I dressed my outside up and didn't let anyone to close. I had learned very well as a child how to pretend that something wasn't what it was to keep people from knowing what was going on inside me.

Growing up with street knowledge and hustlers all around me and in my family helped me find a way to my path of self destruction quickly. I wasn't drinking because I vowed to myself when I was ten I would never drink; that was from watching the adults around me actions when they were drinking. I wasn't doing drugs because I didn't want anything to alter my mind frame while in the trap; I also saw what it did to people and I did not want to end up like that.

My addiction was money and power to get what I wanted, when I wanted it, from whom I wanted it from. If you didn't have money and cars I couldn't really waste my time because I needed someone that could help me get out of the game what I needed at that time.

I often would talk to boys who were not in the game just to get away from the street life sometimes. This was a case of my mind being twisted with confusion. I wanted what I wanted from the streets but it often gave you things you really didn't want to deal with. The older I got the more I learned; and the more I learned I mastered how to block feelings and keep my eyes on my prize or what I thought was the prize at that time (money, partying and men).

I started feeling real funny inside. Something was driving me into change and I could not escape it, but I was trying to ignore it. But, my conscious was on watch for my life, and I was always aware of my surroundings. I knew at anytime something could go wrong I felt it, I just didn't take heed to it. I was walking amongst men with dead souls and those who were lost to the streets far deeper than me. So I had to keep my eyes open and ears clear.

~~LIFE'S LESSONS COMES IN MANY WAYS. ESPECIALLY IN THE STREETS THOSE LESSONS CAN LEAD YOU TO THE SHADOWS IN THE VALLEY OF DEATH!

I had taken my buddies to pick up a package. I sat in the car while they went in to get it. It was taking longer than I thought so I got out the car to see what the hold up was. I heard noises so I peeked into a window and the things my eyes saw, made my stomach turn. It was a hold up alright, people were tide up.

If a demon could walk with power without a body or not being connected to a soul it would be a fierce one to reckon with wondering this earth. But because demons have to be connected to a soul to gain its power to do its most damage, it seeks out the right one. I don't think this demon backed down until it met its match in human form; my so called street buddy.

I looked at his eyes and it scared me. My grandmother us to always tell me, you can tell a lot by a person's eyes. His eyes at that moment, told a tale of legends of demons standing up strong in human form. I ran and got in the car, I guess they saw me because they ran out of the house; as they jumped in I saw someone coming out.

Just like that! Just in a moments time my whole world could have changed, by being with the wrong people, in a wrong place. I was being set up by satan. Not even knowing that road was chosen and sent by him to take me down; giving me a one way ticket straight from hell to jail or my fleshly death. That's why we have to always be careful of the company we keep no matter what our circumstances may be. Choices mean your life! Some of the most important issues I have been faced with were based on choices, both good and bad ones. This was a bad one! A life altering decision! This had hindered my flesh!

(2NDCORINTHIANS 12 VS 7-10): AND LEST I SHOULD BE EXALTED ABOVE MEASURE BY THE ABUNDANCE OF THE REVELATIONS, A THORN IN THE FLESH WAS GIVEN TO ME, A MESSENGER OF SATAN TO BUFFET ME, LEST I BE EXALTED ABOVE MEASURE. CONCERNING THIS THING I PLEADED WITH THE LORD THREE TIMES THAT IT MIGHT DEPART FROM ME. AND HE SAID TO ME, "MY GRACE IS SUFFICIENT FOR YOU, FOR MY STRENGTH IS MADE PERFECT IN WEAKNESS." THEREFORE MOST GLADLY I WILL RATHER BOAST IN MY INFIRMITIES, THAT THE POWER OF CHRIST MAY REST UPON ME. THEREFORE I TAKE PLEASURE IN INFIRMITIES, IN REPROACHES, IN NEEDS, IN PERSECUTIONS, IN DISTRESSES, FOR CHRIST'S SAKE. FOR WHEN I AM WEAK, THEN I AM STRONG.

REAL TALK:

I was out of sight out of mind! I had seen a lot of things being one of the girls (considering I felt like I was one of the boys) with a group of boys who had made themselves hustlers, pimps, players and drug dealers of the streets.

This one specific one was like the devil himself walking the earth. He used to always say he would not see the age 21 and he didn't. I had seen him escape car wrecks; literally get out of the car after just being in a high speed chase with the cops and take off running. I had seen this same guy (who I said a demon in its rare form) kick out the police car window; after beating up the cop and start running with handcuffs on. But seeing a baby being a pawn and its life being in danger like that made me even more angry and sick to my stomach. This time I was angry at what was happening around me. I was angry at myself for allowing that person to be apart of my life. What if someone did that to my babies? With my mind frame at that time of my life, it would have caused a major problem in this universe. Nothing could have saved me or them!

I knew it was time to go! I had to get out of the streets it was no longer a productive asset for me it was making my soul deteriorate more and making me fall into another realm of destruction. Things were already dangerous and really not getting safer. I didn't know who I had become but I knew it was not pretty and God was not pleased.

Not only was I in pain I also had stepped into the shadows of death doors. Something my grand mother use to tell me stuck in my mind, even while I was yet in sin; "do unto others as you wish to be done unto you". Even though I turned to the streets thinking it would define me it didn't mean I treated people just foul.

Even though I was on a wrong path did not mean I had no morals at all. I was just lost in a world of sin trying to get back to where I begin, before the womb. Back to the word God spoke over my life! Old people use to tell me "the word can never come back void." Even if the enemy had declared war against me it was not my flesh he was after it was the God in me; it was the words God spoke over my life that he was trying to take hostage and give me no where to escape to.

I didn't want to escape to anyone at this time. I wanted to escape myself and find a place where I could die or recover from the streets. I was fed up! And no-one could do anything about it.

There comes a time and place where you get tired. Once you get tired change must be in sight. Change in your mind and spirit has to take place. At that place people and things had to go and I had to let them go. No matter how hard it may have been I had to let go. They didn't understand my change. So, letting go brought on a lot of hatred towards me it changed faces on me. Because I was changing my life and talking about being into God they laughed at me and teased me.

I had a bond with my street brothers/buddies but I had to let them go. It was one of the hardest things in my life to do. I was so comfortable with them having my back and being around them that I didn't know where to lean anymore.

I had figured out in order to change my life I had to change my surroundings and I had to change my environment. I started letting go of a lot of things, things I didn't feel I was ready to let go, but had to. Letting go caused confusion but I was already lost so why continue to hold on. I didn't know really what to do next. One thing I knew not to do at that time was not to let go of God's hand, be that he stretched it out to me! I was holding on for dear life!

I had money saved up but without money coming in soon what was saved would give out. I started braiding hair and doing smaller things on the side. Once a hustler always a hustler! Life just becomes a different kind of hustle. A legal/safe hustle!

I was focusing more on being a better mother and loving my daughters the way I wanted to be loved. I had, had my second daughter by now. So, I started looking for a job. I didn't know what I wanted to do but I wasn't finding anything that would give me the money I was used to in the streets, so it was hard to settle. I went to school and took up classes trying to get my mind back in books. I had always been very book smart. The paths just crossed at the wrong intersection and I made the wrong turn or a different turn. When I turned I ended up on the wrong road and I got lost in the moments. I was searching for something, which was not apart of my destiny. I began to enjoy the good life; at least what I thought was the good life.

It's hard to pick up and change your road. I realized it's easy to get in trouble but hard to get out. Another thing I realized is, it's hard to do the right things but easy to do the wrong. When you're doing wrong no-one tries to stop you but when you're doing right it always seem like road blocks pop up and people are in your ears playing the enemies partner. It's like a catch twenty-two!

So, at this time I am fighting both worlds. I was in the middle of no man's land; I was cast down on all sides! But I realized though I was cast down I had something in me that was yet unconquered.

2ND CORINTHIANS 4 VS 8-9: WE ARE HARD PRESSED ON EVERY SIDE, YET NOT CRUSHED; WE ARE PERPLEXED, BUT NOT IN DESPAIR; PERSECUTED, BUT NOT FORSAKEN; STRUCK DOWN, BUT NOT DESTROYED-

I was always told <u>what don't kill me makes me stronger!</u> That stayed on my mind! I use to wish it just killed me, because the pain and misery was too much to bear. In order to save my life I had to give up my life and give it back to the rightful owner. I had to give my life back to its rightful owner so that he could make the pain go away! And cover you in the shadows of death!

People, it's time to give your life back to the rightful owner! It's time to repent of your sins and rededicate your life back to the one who predestined you and foreknew you, so you can find where the pain lies and allow him to lead you back to the path of righteousness.

CHAPTER FOUR

<u>MANIFISTATION OF</u>

<u>THE PAIN</u>

<u>(M-P)</u>

EVERYTHING THAT PAIN MANIFESTED; FIRST STARTED IN DARKNESS BEHIND LIFES TRAGEDIES. THAT THING THAT ROARS COMES FROM THE INSIDE OF YOU AND IF IT'S NOT RELEASED YOU BLOW A FUSE AND WONDER WHAT'S NEXT! IF YOU FIGUE OUT, REVEAL AND ACCEPT WHAT'S IN YOU WEIGHING YOU DOWN IT WILL HELP BRING FORTH THE MANIFISTATION OF THE REAL YOU THAT COMES AFTER THE PAIN!

IT'S TIME TO SWITCH GEAR AND CHANGE ROADS! WE ARE GOING SOMEWHERE SO HOLD ON!

(MAIN ENTRY)

Money was funny trying to change my ways. I had been looking for a job and I had not found one so I began to take some more classes to keep my mind off the streets. I was trying to do things a little different so that my kids did not have to suffer as much as I did. I wanted to raise my daughters better so I turned over a new lease.

I was determined to change my occupation. I wanted to change my view of having a man. That man thing didn't work well with me. I am not one that sits around and acts as if nothing is going on no matter what a person is doing for me. You can pay all the bills, you can buy me and give me the world; I still will not allow you to run over me and disrespect me.

I always felt respect was and is a very important asset to give to a person and if you don't have respect for someone you will do just about anything to them. You learn things like that in street life one on one! Because being in the streets you had to stand your grounds for respect.

I tried to be with someone where it was really a real relationship. We were doing things together and discussing life, but I wasn't going to let my dignity of a woman be put on the line for a man.

I got pregnant and I guess that was a part of Gods plan even with the enemy still on the prowl with his own plan to break me. I had a birth control in my arm that they were trying out, I guess. Because it along with other birth controls didn't work on me and at that time it felt almost impossible to be absent from it. So, now I am pregnant again. How do you change course when you try to prevent it? My grandmother told me everything happens for a reason! Hum!

This pregnancy was different from my daughters. I was very sick and the doctor put me on bed rest early on. So he (that boyfriend) decided to do what ever he liked. He started not coming home, messing with all type of women and just being very disrespectful with how he was doing things.

Even though he was in the streets it did not give him a pass to handle things any kind of way. He was in the streets hustling before I got pregnant and things were not like that so what happened? Street life, what do you do with it! Darned if you do darned if you don't! It's a whole other world of its own and if you aren't careful it sucks you dry.

Time was really flying; I was about five or six months pregnant, my hormones were on over load and my emotions were distorted. Emotionally, I really couldn't handle everything he was putting me through so I broke. This was the first time I was in a physical altercation in a relationship, maybe because I ran from relationships trying to escape that.

My anger and my lashing out caused things to fester from my past and instead of him being the abuser, I was. I was enraged and he was in fear for his life, but he refused to leave. I wanted him to leave my apartment but he wouldn't. I wanted him to just leave me alone but he wouldn't. I didn't understand if you're not happy and you wanted other people why not just leave. I was miserable! In my mind I was gone from him he was just still there for what ever reason. It was an emotional rollercoaster! I didn't trust him as far as I could see him. My little sister was living with me to go to school and she wasn't acting right. His presence was not helping her to do better! Things were already off balance in her life and she was fighting a battle that was dragging her down. She was in a place where she didn't understand her pain.

I kept telling him as soon as I have this baby I was out. I don't know if he thought I was kidding or what, but I wasn't! My mind was made up. I was to far gone with more anger and pain. This pain had poured over open wounds that had not healed from my past. This was dangerous pain and someone was liable to get hurt. So, I knew I had to go!

I sat back and waited. He continued to take care of the financial part and had people to come over to clean up. He also gave an associate of mine money to give me a baby shower. But I was a woman scorned and there was nothing that he could have done to change my mind. I continued to wait in the mist of more drama!

Finally, my first son came on my grandmother's birthday. He was about three and a half weeks early, probably because of all the stress I had been going through. After I saw that he was fine and healthy I
Was glad he was here. I always wanted a son and finally I got one, even if it was with someone I felt was the wrong person; after the fact. But, God chose wisely the right father for my son. I thought I knew, but who paid me to think. People are not always who we want them to be. After a while it's like a twist in their personality, then your whole world changes and by then you have already given yourself to them.

I figured out change is only good if you first empty what had you held up so you can make a more conscious decision or choice. I had not emptied myself of my past life issues so I dangled in a circle of bad choices based on misinformation that I had allowed myself to get from the world and from the streets.

That time was a blow to my emotional state and it was time for me to move on with my life. It was easy for me to just pick up and leave a man because as I watched my mother relationship with the man with the iron fist, over the years she would never leave and the outcome of it was not good to me. So I did not want to sit around and waste years of my life with someone that was no longer productive for me or that hindered my spirit more than it already was. I just couldn't waste that energy if the results weren't going to end with some hope for tomorrow.

I had to do something! A friend of mine had told me about her job and that they would be hiring soon. It was at a club and she said they made good money off tips. I recovered for about four weeks and I went and applied for the job. I got an interview right then and was hired. I was so happy because I didn't want to go back to the streets hustling but I was not going to stay in that toxic relationship. I didn't need anything else to be poured over my already open wounds.

I had been praying and asking God to help me get a job that will financially support me so that I can leave him. I didn't understand stepping out on faith at that time but God knew what I had gone through with my son's father during my pregnancy. He knew I was trying very hard to change but change didn't want to try hard with me.

GALATIANS 6 VS 7: DO NOT BE DECIEVED, GOD IS NOT MOCKED; FOR WHATEVER YOU SOW, THAT YOU SHALL ALSO REAP.

I know he saw I was really trying to change; that I was a babe in the spiritual world trying to escape the street life. God had to know that change was not easy for me.

He spared me once again and opened up a door where I could make enough money to take care of my kids and household without help from the streets because all I knew was the streets, and I knew people that could help bring me that fast money!

God helped me begin a new journey, a new chapter in my life. I stepped into another part of this world; the club life. The night life! How do you escape from it! One way or another it clings to you and captivate your soul!

Thank God I had been clubbed out by this time. I had been going to them since I was fifteen years old. I was at teenage clubs, skating rinks and I was getting into adult clubs early! Money is power! It also talks you right into the best clubs and V.I.P! I have had V.I.P status for a while in the club life by being in the street life, it no longer thrilled me.

I began working at club 112 which was one of the hottest clubs going on in Atlanta around this time. This was the place to be for everyone that was into the club scene. It didn't faze me because I didn't look at the club life like everyone else; to me club life was capitalism, in my eyes anyway. I was there for the sole purpose of making money to take care of my kids and my household.

JOURNEY TO MY LIFE @ CLUB 112 (1995-2000): I had never worked at a club before but I gave it a try. My hours were good I could be a mother all day put my kids to sleep with a baby sitter which was always family; my little cousins, my sisters or my daughter's god-mother. I would go to work and be home before they woke up. That I enjoyed so much!

When you're in the street life your job was all day and night and then you would have to not answer the phone to give all of yourself to your kids. It wears you out. I thought about dancing (stripping) but it wasn't for me. It wares you out physically, and what they make off one dance I would make triple in minutes time, with what I had going on. I give my hats off to anyone that's able to do that because your mind and body have to withstand a lot. Besides, I knew too many people, had too many uncles and cousins in the night life for that to be my job. Even though what I was doing was more of a risk I'd rather do that than stripping and selling my body. Not knocking another woman's hustle because I know women in the streets do what we feel we have to do at that moment to survive, eat and make ends meet.

It would have been just too much for me. Besides I didn't like people looking at me like that or touching on me unless I wanted them to.

So I followed other paths. Never in a million years would I have ever thought I would become a waitress because I thought I was beyond that. But I figured you have to start somewhere. I hadn't worked a job other than a summer job at camp when I was fifteen and at burger king when I was pregnant with my first daughter trying to get out of the streets. I was twenty two with three kids and I was not trying to turn back or let them live a life of lack. I was already living, walking, and breathing pain which had me on paths and battle fields that weren't mine to begin with.

****Realize and understand, people can never understand your pain if they have never walked in your shoes! They say they wouldn't be like you or me. How do they know! Just what if! What they should always realize and know is circumstances are handled by the level of a persons mind. What the person perceives to be right may come from what they hold dear in the levels of their mind! This will tell how a person responds to life's issues when they are face to face with pain or tragedy!

~**The new journey begins:** Club 112 was an awesome place to work despite of the craziness that took place? When I started working there I had to build my section up. The more regular customers you have the more money you make. I was feeling the place out trying to figure out what works for me and what didn't. On the table sat a sign that said "two drink minimum." I never realized why clubs had those until I started working at one. If people are sitting and not drinking you can't serve anyone so you don't make tips. I was glad that was there when I started getting regular customers. It gave me the right to let them set down and for those not drinking to get up. I didn't mind them sitting there I wasn't mean and nasty I just let them know that later these tables would be filled with stars or special customers placed by my bouncers.

One night probably a month after working there I was walking to the bar to get someone a drink and there was a group of guys standing against the wall. I asked them did they need anything they said yes I took their orders and when I came back with their drinks they asked me how they could find a seat. They said the other waitresses had turned them away, so I let them sit in my section. That night they ordered so much and tipped me very well. I was so happy I stopped for them! Life lesson; never pass a good thing by because of how it looks.

Come to find out they were visiting from Miami. They asked me to save them a table for the next night which was Saturday, one of our best nights for making money; but I did! I made beyond the quota I had set for myself that night. One of the guys out of that group had been trying to talk to me the night before, and all that night. Before he left he gave me a paper with four numbers on it. He was so respectful and I liked his personality. I just did not feel like going through anything else at that time with a man. I was still trying to get over the mess I went through with my son's father. But, he was persistent so I gave in to him. I was glad I did; he was a very special person in my life. He helped me to understand things I thought I had pushed away from my mind.

    Anyway, after that night my section blew up. I guess the bouncers saw I was going to make money with or without them. When you are the new person you are last in line to get good tipping customers. When I started I was along the wall it was hard to make money over there but I did; once a hustler always a hustler it just becomes a different way of hustling. When a waitress is fired or quit the next in line gets a better spot. At this time my section was by V.I.P right at the dance floor. I liked my section being there. The only way I wanted to move was to go to V.I.P which I was next in line for.

    Anyway, I begin to realize people really don't know you or where you come from but they judge you off what you are doing and were you are at and who they think they are over you. I waited on a lot of famous people at 112, especially in the music industry. Some where very nice and tipped good but there were some that did not tip well and weren't pleasant to deal with. This was a shame!

Sometimes you expect more out of people but you can't! You can only expect what they give to you and decide if you will deal with it or not. For some reason or another I have always been in a circle where I was connected to famous people or well known people. They always taught me life lessons.

    One of the first cool ones I waited on was Trech and Pepper. They didn't act untouchable they were very down to earth they seemed very happy and full of positive energy. Another one that was down to earth was (LL Cool J). One night he came in, my manager came to me and said he would be sitting in my section for a while. That night I had been waiting on one of my regular customer to come that tips me a lot. I was not really up for it because I had already made arrangements for my section. I was there to make money and learn life lessons to get me to my next level. I was not up to be in the face of famous/well known people.

When he came over he said he does not drink. In my mind I thought "I will not be making money tonight." He ordered a fruit drink mixed with pineapple juice. While he was there everyone was crowding my section and trying to get by his body guards. It was horrible trying to get through the crowd. The other waitresses were coming over to see LL they wanted to know why I wasn't going crazy. I have always felt as if I had my own famous status so it didn't really move me when famous people were around, they are humans just like me, I needed to make money. That's what I had on my mind. Besides a person status does not say to me if they are famous or not their work in this world and community is what determines if I feel a person stands up to their famous status or not. It's never about your status but what you give to the world to make it better that makes you.

I was standing next to LL and he started talking to me and some how tattoos were brought up and he asked me did I want to see something I said "what?" He had just gotten a tattoo so he took his arm out of his shirt and showed me a microphone going up his arm it was very nice. Right after that the DJ started playing all his old and new songs. He got on the dance floor along with his body guards; because people were trying to bum rush him on the dance floor. He was so down to earth! When he got ready to leave he made his body guards empty their pockets and give me all the money they had in them, because he said he didn't carry cash on him. It really didn't matter if he did or didn't, he was very respectful of me. Besides he only ordered a fruit drink!

Unlike this other person that ordered 30 bottles of Moet and 22 half bottles of Moet, food, and then asked me to take orders from others that were in his group. Yet he did not tip well. One of the other waitresses, who waited on him before, warned me that he didn't tip well. When they set this known Coe/producer of Atlanta (which I will leave unknown) I thought maybe he had an off night with her and he had so much going on that he thought he had taken good care of his waitress. Well I guess that was not the case because out of all that he ordered from me he tipped me twenty two dollars. That was gratuity off two bottles. He had ordered, all of fifty bottles of Moet and a few other things. I was trying to explain to him his tab verse how much he tipped me but he brushed me off.

    I have always told myself that everything in life is a lesson. I also had learned to choose my battles and figure out the lesson. What do you learn from the situation you're encountering? In that situation I learned that no matter how far you get in life if you do not value everyone you come in contact with you miss the purpose God brought them into your presence. I also learned that people might have it all financially but still lack in character, as I had before.

One thing I never did was not give people what they were entitled to and I always made sure who I was with tipped generously and if they didn't I did. I did that before I ever became a waitress because I valued life and money differently. People work hard for their money no matter how small the job looks to others.

I was kind of upset with him by the outcome because I worked hard and made sure he and his people had great service. I felt he should have known better, maybe he didn't. I don't know! But I wondered why he didn't think anything was wrong with that. Maybe one day he would realize even those he looked down on are somebody also. I had to forgive him and not allow that to weigh on my heart. Once a hustler always a hustler so you know I got mine anyway!

    *People go through life without a second thought of the person they may have affected. They never realize that spiritually they are connected to a greater being that brings you into the lives of certain people no matter how small they may seem to them.

I soon realized that even though you are famous and well known does not mean you are secure with yourself. One night at work I walked in the kitchen to give an order and another Coe/artist whom I will not mention was using the bathroom in there. The cook was fussing with the other waitresses to get out and stop crowding her kitchen and they were saying they wanted to see him. She said "I don't care who he is, everyone, but Gan needs to get out of my kitchen." He came out of the bathroom buckling his belt saying "who dissing me?"

That really threw me off, because I would have never thought that he would care what someone had to say about him. One thing he made me realize was no matter how much you have material wise and wealth wise if you don't truly understand yourself or know your inner man, others would always be able to define who you are.

Just because you have the voice or boldness to speak on something somebody said about you does not make you look like a man or woman it shows your weakness. You should never to allow someone else's words or actions to take you out of your character or define who you are! We should never show someone that what they say holds value in your thoughts. ****Real talk to understand: the most important thing is finding yourself deep down within the rebels of life to define who you truly are. Once defined, no matter what people say or how people react to you, you will never allow it to affect you negatively; no matter if you have wealth or not. **"For what profit is it to a man if he gains the whole world, and loses his own soul? Or what will a man gives in exchange for his soul? Mathew 16 vs. 26.**

Working at club 112, allowed me to see a lot of things and meet a lot of different people. The club life is a fast lane. You can see a lot of things and be in the mist of a lot of different situations. On one of the busiest nights at 112 I saw another life changing scene. The crowd was over bearing and things were wild. There were so many people standing in the V.I.P line and the regular line was wrapped around the building. As I was standing outside looking for one of my customers to get them through the gate, some people tried to bum rush the line. When that was done it caused an up roar with security and the officers at the club took over. The officers were trying to get things under control and as they pushed the line back an artist was pushed against a window and the window shattered leaving a piece of glass in her back. There was so much confusion security really couldn't chance any disorder because things would have been out of control and more people could have gotten hurt.

I never condoned what happened with the artist but that incident put the club in a bad state when it was not directly the club who was involved in the situation at hand. This disturbance ended up on the news and on radio stations which caused a great fall in 112's business. Negative words from a person of status cause a chain reaction of negative outcomes. I really felt bad for her because of all the things that followed behind this incident. But it teaches you a great life lesson; sometimes it's best to be quiet until things can get in order or the commotion is ceased then try a better approach.

I have learned in the mist of mess silence is the best tool. If you stay humble the results of your outcome would be better for your circumstances. Humbleness is the best tool in the mist of issues. **"Assuredly, I say to you, unless you are converted and become as little children, you will by no means enter the kingdom of heaven. 'Therefore whoever humbles himself as this little child is the greatest in the kingdom of heaven." Mathew 18 vs. 36-4.**

I used to hear older people say as I was growing up, that God gave us two ears and one mouth so that we can do more listening and less talking. I think that makes a lot of sense. What we have less of can be heard louder. Silence is more deadly than words in my experience, especially with men.

Anyway, 112 had some awesome DJ's. One of my favorite ones was Chris Luva, Luva (Ludicris). He was such a role model. Every time I saw him he was smiling and talking positive. I would always take the DJ's something to drink when they couldn't leave the booth. A lot of the waitresses didn't do this. I didn't mind I was transforming into a mind of humbleness.

He would always tell me about his music; what he wanted to do and was going to do. He was a prime example of speaking things into existence even when you are being doubted. Words are powerful and they carry weight. Just think how much power comes behind speaking, believing and moving on it. Who can stop the process other than yourself? **Examine what you speak before you release it. If you don't want it to happen don't speak it. We bring so much on ourselves by our words and don't realize it. We are creating our circumstances by the things we speak and focus on the most.**

After that altercation business had slowed down. Money was short all types of things were going on with trying to make money. There was something stirring up inside me that wouldn't rest. I began to look for another job because I just didn't know what to expect.

There goes that shift again! It was time for a new journey and another chapter for my life. God has a way of changing your circumstances even if you're not ready for them to be changed. He has a way of shutting down a road you keep trying to make stay open.

(NOBODY ELSE TO HOLD ON TO)

Never under estimate the power of lose. Business was slow at the club. I had recently gotten a house, then bam! Things went sour. I started questioning maybe it wasn't time for me to get it. Maybe I stepped out of the will of God again and upset him. I don't know but, just as I was trying to live right and do right all hell broke lose. I did not want to go back on my promise to God about leaving the street life. I didn't know what else to do I didn't want to not have or not be able to feed my kids.

hell seems to have no fear, it will try to take you down!

One day I was at work, this company delivered the furniture I ordered. They were supposed to assemble the items, but they just sat the boxes against the wall. I had just come in from work and picking up my kids. So I put things down and tried to get the kids ready for a bath. While I was getting things together, my son was playing with his truck on the floor. He was not bothering anything, he was right across from me, and I heard him making noise as he pushed his truck. The next thing I know I heard a loud noise and my baby started crying. The mirror that goes on the big dresser drawer had fallen on him. I called for an ambulance, when they came they said he was alright. The ambulance service told me to put ice on his knee and make him move around in the morning and left.

Well morning came and he could not get up. I looked at his leg and it looked like something was dangling on the inside. I got in my car and rushed to the hospital. When they did an x-ray his femur bone (which is the thigh bone; one of the biggest bone in the body), was broken along with a tare in his hip bone.

Once they told the doctor the outcome in walks a social worker. She started asking questions about child abuse. I was so upset and crying. My mom was telling me to just calm down. I told them to call the ambulance company and ask them why they didn't bring us to the hospital last night and get out my face. They left out made the call, then came back in and apologized to me. They tried everything to make it right but they had sent me into another world. There were two things you didn't mess with in my life; the love I had for my children and my money.

I think one of the hardest things in the world as a mother is seeing your child in pain. That day they had to put my son who was only two years old, on a traction machine to pull the bones back in place. I think I cried more than he did. He was so brave. He said "mommy I am alright." I did not want him to see that I was hurting and upset, but he could always tell. He was very smart for his age and still is. He always knew if something was wrong and he would tell me "God will take care of it mommy."

Once he was in traction he was also put in a full body cast from chest to feet. He could no longer get around so I had to care for him as a little baby all over again. I even had to start putting diapers on him. It was a major test and trial. I had just had my second son some months prior and his father was in another state. I had to send my baby there for a while in order to take care of Ez, while he was in the body cast. This was one of the hardest things I felt I had to do but I did what I felt were best for that entire situation.

Now I could not work, so no income would be coming in. I had chosen to be the sole provider for my kids and me. I did not like drama nor did I like to beg anyone for anything.

Everything spiraled out of control. What do I do? I felt hopeless and helpless. Then I got news that my son father was in jail in another state. The income from him went down hill. He had to handle personal matters which caused everything to be held up. Nothing would open up financially. Nothing! Who would have thought, all doors would shut!

One day I got a phone call stating that my biological father was in the hospital. The social worker at the hospital told me he needed someone to take him in and they would get him a nurse when he got released. I did not have the means to help; I was losing my house. I did not know what would be my next step. I tried to figure a way to help him. But about two weeks later the hospital called and said they didn't know if he was going to make it.

I remember going to see him and he looked over at me and smiled and when he smiled tears started running down his face. The same smile I remembered when I was a little girl. The same smile that made me know I was daddy's little girl.

He couldn't speak because he had a stroke. Seeing him like that hurt me so badly, because I couldn't do anything for him. It was bad enough that he had been sent to another home and we where not notified after his mother passed in 1993. We hadn't seen him in years, and when we were notified, he's on his death bed. The nursing home had let him wandered off ill and he had gotten frost bitten and had several strokes back to back. That's why no matter what, we should always love. People need others to help them up hills and mountains and through valley lows if not God would not have created woman for man. He said "it is not right for man to be alone."

My son was still in a body cast, I was trying to make money, my father was in the hospital and I was fighting to save my house. I had been trying to just stand. I was holding on for dear life to save myself. I was lying on the floor of my living room and I was looking at the word channel and Juanita Bynum was speaking and she said **"WHAT YOU ARE GOING THROUGH IS GOING TO TAKE YOU TO ANOTHER LEVEL WITH GOD! THAT YOU ARE BEING SET UP BY GOD TO RECEIVE YOUR GREATEST DESTINY."** I just started crying and crying and tears would not stop and I heard God say to me "don't you worry I am preparing you for greater levels in the kingdom. If you can make it through this you can make it through anything." I told God "I don't think I can make it because I was under attack from a spiritual level and nothing in this world was helping me". He said "yes you can, I have a promise for you that will release things beyond your imaginations." I heard a pastor say one day "God does not give you a promise on the level you are on, and he doesn't give you a promise you can't reach." I got off the floor went to sleep and when I woke up I began to pack. I decided that if I was going to move forward it was time for me to let go.

As I was packing I got a call that my father had passed. I had to plans his funeral because there was no one else to do it. By this time I was just too messed up, but I was still holding on! I don't know what to but I was holding on. My aunt bought him a suit. She picked me up with someone she new from a funeral home so that I could pick out his casket and burial sight. His mother had one near her so that's the one he was laid to rest in. It was so hard to view his body and make sure everything was fine with my children.

I was still holding on! I felt God had me hostage! I thought it was the enemy at first; but I figured, the only way these chain of events would happen, was if God allowed it to. Test, suffering, afflictions and adversities had come upon me. My spirit had to shift and the only way to move me to another level was to push me into it. I guess I wasn't getting there on my own fast enough. God left it so that I could not find what I needed in anyone but him. I had no one to turn to for help. Another part of God's great master plan!

At this point I was gasping for air with the determination that I would not give in. I was lost to devastation. I felt like I had died a thousand deaths at one time by the trials and struggles that had been put there to destroy my mind. I felt the darkness had snatched me back beneath the rubble where I once was.

Some time had past by and I was trying to get my head together. I was trying to find a place to move to because I was living with my daughter's God-mother. I had found a day job and gone back to work at 112 but at the door. I was still pressing, until three months later my grandfather went to the hospital because a branch had fallen on his back some weeks prior and it was still hurting. He hated going to the doctor and always tried remedies but they weren't working. When they ran test they said he had colon and prostate cancer. There was nothing the doctors could do, we were told to take him home and help him to be as comfortable as possible! He went to my aunt's house and I didn't want to see him like that. I was hurting already hurting inside, another blow! How strong did God want me, I asked myself?

I was really hurt! I had lost enough that year I thought but some higher power didn't think it was enough. I finally went to see him and held his hands and sat looking into space. I just didn't understand what was going on. I had just lost all the worldly materials I had, my father and now this. The next day I received a call saying he was gone. I was so angry I felt everyone gave up on him. But my anger was made up of a lot of things but I could only see one. I was his Gan baby! He was my granddaddy!

I just didn't want to accept that the one man who made sure I was alright and made me feel special was gone. The one man in my life that never left me or turned his back on me was gone. It was over! I had nothing left in me! Several nights before his death I had a dream; first I saw my granddad lying down on this bed of flowers. Then the scene changed and he was calling me from a back room with bright lights and as I tried to get to him the further away he would become, yet his voice seemed close. When I looked in his casket there he was with the same thing he had on in the dream I had before he past. I was not in the church long; I had to be carried out; I couldn't breath and I couldn't stop crying. You know, that was the first time I had seen my grandfather in a church. Isn't that ironic!

Life has away of dealing you a hand that I would call a flush. What can you really do with the chain of events that is released on you? Do you strategize and try to win the war; before a battle takes place within? I began to think I was losing but what was really going on in me was I was being broken. I was being whooped by God! I was trying to fight for my directions. I had taken a step to change my life but life started fighting back. I realized I had not let go of a lot of things and those things hindered my growth spiritually. Once you start to change your life you have to change your mind and once you change your mind you have to empty all the mess that was left behind.

I began to be weary, I began to lose strength, and I begin to ask how could God allow all these things to take place? He saw that I was trying so hard to live right and change my life? It was a battle amongst spiritual principalities going on inside of me. It felt like the enemy was sending darts of fire at me, trying to keep me out of the will of God. He saw that I was moving away from him and the grounds he governed into the grounds God had dominion over. I needed the right equipment to stand while under attack. I read something that touched me: **PUT ON THE WHOLE ARMOR OF GOD, THAT YOU MAY BE ABLE TO STAND AGAINST THE WILES OF THE DEVIL. FOR WE DO NOT WRESTLE AGAINST FLESH AND BLOOD, BUT AGAINST PRINCIPALITIES, AGAINST POWERS, AGAINST THE RULERS OF THE DARKNESS OF THIS AGE, AGAINST SPIRITUAL HOSTS OF WICKEDNESS IN THE HEAVENLY PLACES. EPHESIANS 6VS 11-12.**

I wondered if you had not fully gained the knowledge of the whole armor of God what do you do? Do you give up or do you find what's left to hold on to?

I felt I had nothing left to hold on to. I was dying inside and no-one could help me, nor heal my pain. The whole armor did not seem relevant to me because I did not understand it yet! How do you put on this armor?

PHILLIPPEANS 1 VS 20-21: ACCORDING TO MY EARNEST EXPECTATION AND HOPE THAT IN NOTHING I SHALL BE ASHAMED, BUT WITH ALL BOLDNESS, AS ALWAYS, SO NOW ALSO CHRIST WILL BE MAGNIFIED IN MY BODY, WHETHER BY LIFE OR DEATH. FOR TO ME, TO LIVE IN CHRIST AND TO DIE IS GAIN. At one point I felt if I had to go through all this pain and lose everything what would I gain. My hair was falling out and I was losing weight. I didn't have an appetite. I held on to nothing, thinking God yet again gave up on me. Even in those thoughts I continued to press as I worked on being obedient unto His words, even if it killed me.

(OBEDIENT TO THE POINT OF DEATH)

Often it felt like being obedient was causing parts of me to die. Death was taking hold of who I was in the mist of the darkness that was untouched. I soon found out it was not about me but about what God was teaching me.

PHILLIPIANS 2 VS 7 & 8: BUT MADE HIMSELF OF NO REPUTATION, TAKING THE FORM OF A BONDSERVANT, AND COMING IN THE LIKENESS OF MEN. AND BEING FOUND IN APPERANCE AS A MAN; HE HUMBLED HIMSELF AND BECAME OBEDIENT TO THE POINT OF DEATH, EVEN THE DEATH OF THE CROSS.

I have always had these dreams since I was a little girl. They are dreams about things and people. Soon, what I dreamed would manifest some how. It used to be so scary and I thought I was cursed or crazy. I just couldn't tell anyone about my dreams because I thought they would look at me crazy. The few I did tell surely looked at me crazy, except for my grandmother. Those that called me their friends in the flesh had already scorned me to be crazy. Especially, after I was trying to change my life. The more I proclaimed God to be my father and my children's father, the more they called me crazy. I knew I was always different, but it was hidden from their eyes.

The older I got the more the dreams enhanced. The closer I got to God the more things I saw and heard in the spirit about the world. God would reveal things to me about people, their bodies, and things going on in their spirits. Those things started holding my mind bound because I wasn't releasing it to their spirits. A thousand deaths I felt I was dying! I had already died in the mist of the world being emptied, yet things remained buried inside.

One night I had one of my dreams this time it was concerning me. In it I saw the Garden of Eden on my back. There was no one walking in it, it was a powerful light shining over it and I appeared in the middle of a bed of flowers. Shortly after that I had a dream where I walked into a room where there was a bright light. I looked over to the right and a bed was sitting there in the room, on the bed was a girl cut up into small pieces. The pieces were lying in a pool of blood. I started walking toward the bed and tears started running down my face and a man appeared and the man was the rock. He stretched his arm out to me and I laid in his arm weeping. When I looked up there were boxes with gift wrapping paper. The body pieces were being placed in the box by another man that was in the room. I was crying and crying in my sleep. When I woke up tears were coming down my face. I immediately started talking with God and finally he answered me.
FOR THE LIFE OF THE FLESH IS IN THE BLOOD; AND I HAVE GIVEN IT TO YOU UPON THE ALTAR TO MAKE ATONEMENT FOR YOUR SOULS; FOR IT IS THE BLOOD THAT MAKES ATONEMENT FOR THE SOUL. LEVITICUS 17 VS. 11.
He told me "the little girl was me that I was washed in the blood and the broken pieces were the parts in me that had to be broken and die. The rock symbolized who God was to me during those worldly deaths (and he still is my rock). Also the boxes that were gift wrapped are the gifts he will restore upon me after the storms." He goes on to say "everything I had lost, everything that has been taken from me, every pain I went through was not done in vain it's coming back a hundredfold." **ZECHARIAH 9 VS 11-12: "AS FOR YOU ALSO, BECAUSE OF THE BLOOD OF YOUR COVENANT, I WILL SET YOUR PRISONERS FREE FROM THE WATERLESS PIT. RETURN TO THE STRONGHOLD, YOU PRISONERS OF HOPE EVEN TODAY I DECLARE THAT I WILL RESTORE DOUBLE TO YOU."**

I called a spiritual friend of mine to tell her my dream and she immediately said some of the same things God said to me.

God brings people in your life for a season, reason, or life time. When things begin to die in you people become dead weight. They are no longer on your level and they begin to clash because the spirits can't mix. They don't understand your walk and they question who you are. They become the ones that bound you by your past, while God has already forgiven you of it and moved you to your today's. I had to gain spiritual friends and associates that represented what I was pressing to.

The world mixed with the enemy will force you out of the will of God, your creator. I had learned how to continue to press pass the pain. I had learned how to get up dust off and keep moving no matter what. I had to learn how to stay in prayer even when I didn't want to pray, or thought it wasn't helping. **MATHEW 26 VS 41: "WATCH AND PRAY, LEST YOU ENTER INTO TEMPTATION. THE SPIRIT INDEED IS WILLING, BUT THE FLESH IS WEAK."**
1ST THESSALONIANS 5 VS 17-18: PRAY WITHOUT CEASING, IN EVERYTHING GIVE THANKS; FOR THIS IS THE WILL OF GOD IN CHRIST JESUS FOR YOU.
I had taught myself how to push things out of my mind and heart so that I couldn't feel what was hurting me, so I could keep rising. At least what I thought was rising, I was really falling. I was falling to my death. A spiritual death is more hurtful than death of the body. You feel it all! A spiritual death brings pain as it releases pain, it continues to tear you up inside as it breaks you down from the things the world poured in you. It is happening yet you are still in your flesh standing in a spirit of pain.

(PAIN I BURY YOU UNDER THE PITS OF HELL)

Pain became my best friend, from a little girl. Pain has invaded my space constantly. I use to ask God why so much pain? I didn't ask to be here yet I spent many days in tears. If we were to ever understand the position of pain we can change our condition to gain what it has for us; through my pain strength arose.

I had fallen so far from my purpose because of pain that I did not feel life was worth living anymore. Until, I learned more about my lord and savior.

Our lord carried his own death sentence (the cross). He carried it upon his back in pain yet still pressing forward. Struggling yet pressing to his destiny knowing what the end would be. He continued to press to the hill with forgiveness in his heart for those that ordered his death. Beaten and scorned he did not move until the blood flowed from him for you. The power that was in him is in me and that power is greater than anything that was holding on to me and holding me back from my destiny.

If we allow pain to rob us of our joy we lose our strength. If we lose our strength we lose our power. If we lose power we bury our knowledge. Attention! Pain causes a chain reaction in our spiritual growth yet enhances our worldly walk. Pain begets pain. Healing begets healing. Love begets love. So when you are in pain you give pain to others without knowing it is pain that we are giving. I didn't know how to love because my heart was confused from pain. I never wished my pain on anyone else. I would never want anyone to feel the things I felt. Too many of us are destroyed in pain and never realize through our pain we gain life. We have to accept it, dismiss it, heal from it, and then replace it with something powerful that allows us to grow and move to higher spiritual levels in life.

Without pain we will not understand someone else's walk. We will not hold compassion for others. Without pain we would be blind to the tricks of the enemy. Without pain we would give up and give in; we would bend until we break. Feel it, learn from it, and rise above it.

TRAVEL MY MIND OF PAIN! As you travel through my mind you will see many things. In between those walls hold secrets beyond your dreams. There is a little girl that you will pass hid between those iron walls with hell peeking around looking for the moment to take her down. Now pain became the pilot of her mind and she began to act out and run to the streets thinking maybe it will take care of her needs. Falling into a different world she began to see things that harmed her. The little girl was no more because she hid inside a dark hole. The streets couldn't hold no babes or I would have become a slave to it. Pain is the name of the big bad bully that began to take over and became my inner child's best friend. Once was quiet and meek, now bold and mean living in another man's bad dream! My mind is held imprisoned by the torturer of my soul from hells gates!

Pain would not allow me to see good days anymore, when my mom would cook dinner for everyone and give others a place to sleep. Pain would not let me see that there were some good days in the mist of many bad ones; it has over shadowed. There was laughter, but those days couldn't exist in my mind; it was washed away by pain!

Dear pain,

Pain I dismiss you I no longer have space for you to be here. You have been my friend long enough you helped me to stand strong and be tough against the world. You also caused me to lash out and deprive myself with doubt. You rose up in me while I was yet waddling in defeat. Pain I was told without you I would not gain my place in my own destiny. So I thank you for your presence, but know some how you must leave. You have walked with me, and then allowed the world to push me into captivity. You have held the chains that bound me to my worst enemy, now I have to destroy what he left, before it destroys me. I know you came to make me strong, but you left me unarmed in the lions den. Pain it was fun while I was yet in sin, but now you have out lasted your time and it must truly end.
Pain I dismiss you today, I no longer want to feel my heart dismayed. Now I have learned how to release you through my tears and the abuse. Pain you have taught me how to not let my soul be free from all the misery. Pain I empty you from me, because the enemy knows you keep me from being free. I have to tell you good bye! I must wipe these tears from my eyes! But I forgive you! Pain I forgive you it wasn't your fault. It was a set up by the life I had to fight. So I thank you for the growth I gained while I was in pain. Thank you for allowing me to be true to my

words, because what ever I felt it was heard. Pain you became the beast in me, you did not back down in misery.

Pain, I commend you because even though you had to die you helped my spirit come alive. You entered in by my flesh and I bury you to the pits of hell from which you came. You can no longer hold me by those chains. You walked with me to hell where I left you and I came back with the keys to my destiny. Every key will release the things the enemy locked up and stole from me, when I was walking in my flesh and living in this world of iniquity.

REAL TALK ~~ In order to escape the claws of pain we have to go to the pain giver; the enemy! We have to revisit the days pain stepped in, and snatch it back out. We have to go back to the place where we stopped living and allowed the flesh to invade our spirit. We have to go back to that little girl or boy that lives inside us and tell them we are sorry. Tell them they no longer have to hurt. They no longer have t be scared and full of fear! They no longer have to hide away! Allow them to be that little girl or little boy for moments in your day. Laugh, smile, cry, play and breathe!

That inner child hid because it could not take the pain of what the world was telling him or her. It could not take the pain it was seeing from the world. It could not take care of itself so it had to step down. It could not fight off the enemies, so the inner child had to leave. Your worldly body grew before your inner child had its chance because of life circumstances.

All the imaginations were gone away, that's why life looks so blank. The inner child could no longer see the very thing it wanted to grow up and be! Pain had stepped in; unwanted but necessary!

Pain causes us to make decisions that we later are hurt from or ashamed of. Pain stabs at our soul giving it the push it needs to lose control. It causes us to fall into a deep dark hole that we feel we can't climb out of.

Pain stirs up the emotions and causes turmoil to overtake its space. Why do we need it?

Without pain we will continue to travel in circles and never find a true destination, because our walks will go unappreciated. Without it we would not have anything to fight for or strengthen our spirits! We will not have the strength to fight to the enemy's death in us!

Pain what do we really gain?

1ST CHRONICLES 4 VS 9-10: NOW JABEZ WAS MORE HONORABLE THAN HIS BROTHERS, AND HIS MOTHER CALLED HIS NAME JABEZ, SAYING, "BECAUSE I BORE HIM <u>IN PAIN</u>." AND JABEZ CALLED ON THE GOD OF ISRAEL SAYING, "OH, THAT YOU WOULD BLESS ME INDEED, <u>AND ENLARGE MY TERRITORY, THAT YOUR HAND WOULD BE WITH ME, AND THAT YOU WOULD KEEP ME FROM EVIL, THAT I MAY NOT CAUSE PAIN!</u>" SO GOD GRANTED HIM WHAT HE REQUESTED.

So, I ask you again; pain; what do you get from it! You get to a place in you where you no longer will give out the very thing that held you bound by your past. You gain a warrior breaking lose from the chains, rising and pressing to the newness of your Godly man! You gain you once again; the You before birth! The I Am who I Am before, after, during and in darkness!

*****ROMANS 7 VS 5-6: FOR WHEN WE WERE IN THE FLESH, THE SINFUL PASSIONS WHICH WERE AROUSED BY THE LOW WERE AT WORK IN OUR MEMBERS TO BEAR FRUIT TO DEATH. BUT NOW WE HAVE BEEN DELIVERED FROM THE LAW, HAVING DIED TO WHAT WE WERE HELD BY, SO THAT WE SHOULD SERVE IN THE NEWNESS OF THE SPIRIT AND NOT IN THE OLDNESS OF THE LETTER.

CHAPTER FIVE

QUESTIONING THE FALL OF BABYLON IN ME! (Q-T)

BABYLON MEANING THE UNKNOWN; THE UNKNOWN WILL FALL FROM YOU SO THAT MIRACLES CAN FALL FROM HEAVEN INTO YOUR SPIRIT IF YOU SPEAK IT. MYSTERIES ARE REVEALED LEVEL TO LEVEL; DIMENSION TO DIMENSION.

(QUESTIONING THE POWER OF THE TONGUE)

Quietly speak those things because someone is constantly listening. The power to travel to levels through the power of your tongue and thought is a great mystery. Many times we cause or curse that which belongs to our spirit by speaking things that will force us into the very thing we didn't want to take place. The unknown has been set on high to give us something to fight for in the spirit even as we waddle in the flesh. The walk you walk in the flesh may seem to be the darkest moments and even if they are, it is dark so that you will be driven to bring down the mysteries God has and step into the light. The power of the tongue brings the light!

JAMES 3 VS 5-10: EVEN SO THE TONGUE IS A LITTLE MEMBER AND BOASTS GREAT THINGS, SEE HOW GREAT A FOREST A LITTLE FIRE KINDLES ! AND THE TONGUE IS A FIRE, A WORLD OF INIQUITY. THE TONGUE IS SO SET AMONG OUR MEMBERS THAT IT DEFILES THE WHOLE BODY, AND SETS ON FIRE THE COURSE OF NATURE; AND IT IS SET ON FIRE BY HELL. FOR EVERY KIND OF BEAST AND BIRD, OF REPTILE AND CREATURE OF THE SEA, IS TAMED AND HAS BEEN TAMED BY MANKIND. BUT NO MAN CAN TAME THE TONGUE. IT IS AN UNRULY EVIL, FULL OF DEADLY POISON. WITH IT WE BLESS OUR GOD AND FATHER AND WITH IT WE CURSE MEN, WHO HAVE BEEN MADE IN THE SIMILITUDE OF GOD. OUT OF THE SAME MOUTH PROCEED BLESSING AND CURSING. MY BRETHERN, THESE THINGS OUGHT NOT TO BE SO.

Our tongue holds so much power both positive and negative. We recharge our souls with the things we speak from our mouth and do not even know it. We cause our batteries in our bodies to go dead by that same tongue. Our destiny is left in the unknown land full of mysteries but the words we speak help bring forth that which is unknown to become known at the appointed time.

PROVERBS 18 VS 20- 21: A MAN'S STOMACH SHALL BE SATISFIED FROM THE FRUIT OF HIS MOUTH; FROM THE PRODUCE OF HIS LIPS HE SHALL BE FILLED. 21-DEATH AND LIFE ARE IN THE POWER OF THE TONGUE. AND THOSE WHO LOVE IT WILL EAT ITS FRUIT. (KJV)

I have come to realize that what I speak out of my mouth is carried into a supernatural realm. Once it is exposed power is connected to it to bring it forth. I had to rethink my thoughts in order not to speak the wrong deaths from my tongue.

How can a man speak death over that which God has given life to? Can he curse that which was given to him before he was born? Yes by the very things he allows to flow from his lips. For at birth his breath was breathed in you and he called you therefore he already knew. **JEREMIAH 1 vs. 5: "BEFORE I FORMED YOU IN THE WOMB I KNEW YOU; BEFORE YOU WERE BORN I SANCTIFIED YOU; I ORDAINED YOU A PROPHET TO THE NATIONS".**

I think back on the things people said to me and have done to me; I see that I allowed that to be a part of me when it wasn't suppose to. It was a part of the learning experience in my life but not a part of who I am spiritually. I had allowed too many people's issues and problems to contaminate who I was. I was known by him which breathed the breathe of life in man. His words are so powerful. He spoke and created heaven and earth. Could you ever imagine being on a level spiritually that will allow your words to manifest that which you wish to be released immediately? I began to imagine that; I wanted that!

I was lost while walking in my flesh with the world. I remember speaking or thinking things and seeing them come to past. Those things came from a negative power source. I never understood how until I began my spiritual walk from the flesh. I saw how powerful the tongue was and how our thoughts reveal the connection to our supernatural mind.

The tongue helps us bury that which keeps us alive. So many things in life are spoken to us to kill our spirit, till we suck it in like a sponge and sign the death certificate with our tongue. Then we become that which has been spoken into us instead of that which we truly are. The power of the tongue is deadly if we give energy to that which comes at us.

In order to change our life we have to change the things that we speak. We have to re-train our mind to think those things that are not as though they are. The road is not easy on the journey to find our center in order to become a whole man. The step to becoming a whole man is a process of reconditioning. We have to recondition what we speak, think and how we allow what people say to us to define who we are and hold merit in our minds.

The point where we begin to recondition our mind will show us that in fact our mind is like a sponge and we become that which we soak in and speak from our tongue. **THE PILOT THAT GUIDES US IS LEFT IN THE AIR TO BRING LIFE TO THAT WHICH WAS SENT OUT INTO THE UNIVERSE. WE BECOME THE; I AM IN OUR LIFE.** I am a child of the most high. I am successful. I am! You are what ever you speak or think into your life or spirit. Could you ever imagine something as simple as a thought holding power throughout when released from the tongue?

I have always told my children to speak "I am somebody". If I ask them who are you, they say "I am somebody, I am your angel, I am a queen or for my sons I am a king", "I am a child of God." I constantly speak that to them so their minds could soak it up over the years. I wanted them to have a good habit to hold on to. I want them to speak life into themselves even as children. Always believe that what you say is so!

Allow your words to be a blessing that's spoken into your spirit. **Say it! Believe it!** Wait on the manifestation of it! Continue to speak positive to yourself and those around you who are good or bad. We forget that everyone can change; it just takes a little more time for some. That's why we have to start with self.

*Words to repeat: **I can do all things through Him that keeps me and strengthens me! He that is in me is greater than he that is in the world! I am somebody, I am powerful beyond measure, I am who I am, and I am a child of the Most High! Etc……..**

Continue to feed great thoughts to yourself. Hourly, daily, nightly, continuously!

**** PHILIPPIANS 4 VS. 8: FINALLY, BRETHREN, WHATEVER THINGS ARE TRUE, WHATEVER THINGS ARE NOBLE, WHATEVER THINGS ARE JUST, WHATEVER THINGS ARE PURE WHATEVER THINGS ARE LOVELY, WHATEVER THINGS ARE OF GOOD REPORT IF THERE IS ANY VIRTUE AND IF THERE IS ANYTHING PRAISEWORTHY- MEDITATE ON THESE THINGS.

(REVEALING THE RIGHTEOUS MAN AS)
THE FLESH FALLS

ROMANS 8 VS 29-30: FOR WHOM HE FOREKNEW, HE ALSO PREDESTINED TO BE CONFORMED TO THE IMAGE OF HIS SON; THAT HE MIGHT BE THE FIRST BORN AMONG MANY BROTHEREN; MOREOVER WHOM HE PREDESTINED THESE HE ALSO CALLED; WHOM HE CALLED, THESE HE ALSO JUSTIFIED, AND WHOM HE JUSTIFIED; THESE HE ALSO GLORIFIED.

Have you ever asked yourself who are you? I use to wonder who I was. I really couldn't figure it out! What would I have been had I not been overtaken by pain as a child? What would I have gone through differently if my parents had raised me together and much differently, or had made better choices that involved my well being? Would I have accomplished my career choice of being a lawyer, if someone would have given me a chance? If someone would have looked at me and not seen the outside but was able to discern that my spirit was crying out for help and was dying in pain.

The older I got the more I realized that God does not make mistakes. I was made up genetically and spiritually just as he ordered. I was raised the way he needed me to be to get to the place I ended up at, so that I would have the right tools to stand later in life for what he destined me to stand for. So that I would have the heart and mind to realize someone is going through what I went through or worse and I would be able to help them or minister to them.

I was nourished in the darkness of my mother's womb and was birthed into light. To step back into the eternal light I had to walk in the darkness of the world in order to be rebirth into a new man walking in light.

I walked in the darkness with my flesh over riding my life. My flesh governed that which I did. I woke up thinking what I would do for the day and it was to comfort my fleshly ways. My flesh had confused my inner man, causing me to become blind to its needs. My darkness would become the light in which the inner man would thirst for to form its true being.

I was a righteous man before I was born. Things in my life caused my whole man to be hidden from me. The mystery of the whole man is the mystery that opens up the fight of our life. The enemy seeks to steal that which makes us whole so that we will not hear who is calling us.

If the enemy causes me to close my ears to him whom created me then he starts the fall of whom I'm suppose to be. There are many great falls I have fallen in my life. I used to think the worldly falls were painful. Once I stepped into my spiritual walk my falls were both fleshly painful and spiritually painful.

Inside I was crying because I couldn't breath; the world was suffocating me from the corruption I had stepped into from this world. What I didn't know was that my spirit will rise from beneath the rebels and pain, and give a new life to my inner man. If my flesh man had never risen up in me I would have never understood how to rise above defeat.

As I emptied the world from my mind a battle begin to rise. The battle was me moving from one life style (the flesh) into another (my inner man, my soul). The enemy saw me changing and he was not pleased. When he became angry he began to declare a war for my life greater than he did when I was a child.

He feared that which was rising in me and saw that he could no longer keep me in bondage. Every day I woke up he became upset and tried to knock me back down. What he did not know; I was getting back to where my inner little girl was consumed by the world and that was where he would be domed. My inner child was still holding on to her dreams from that place were she was free.

I realized the deeper the battle the greater the fall would be; back to the place where that little girl hid. If I had to fight to get back to her to find me to uncover our destiny then it was time to defeat the battles so that I could conquer the war.

When the battles would become painful to the point I could not stand anymore, I lay in my bed and cried out endlessly in prayer. My soul kneeled down inside me to seek God's face but something was trying to block me this particular day. My soul was seeking the presence of him who created me. Yet Babylon (the unknown of my flesh) was happening and my soul did not want to be in the mist of the fall. My flesh, my heart, my mind was being broken and my inside felt like I was dying all over. My soul would not get up or look up, until the fall of Babylon (my flesh) took place. During the fall of Babylon (my flesh) a lot of long suffering took place inside and around me.

My body was affected. My mind was affected. My heart was affected. My spirit was on over load and things around me continued to fall. PSALMS 7 VS 9-11: OH, LET THE WICKEDNESS OF THE WICKED COME TO AN END, BUT ESTABLISH THE JUST; BOR THE RIGHTEOUS GOD TESTS THE HEARTS AND MINDS. MY DEFENSE IS OF GOD, WHO SAVES THE UPRIGT IN HEART. GOD IS A JUST JUDGE, AND GOD IS ANGRY WITH THE WICKED EVERY DAY. PSALM 7 15-16: HE MADE HIS PIT AND DUG IT OUT, AND HAS FALLEN INTO THE DITCH WHICH HE MADE. IIS TROUBLE SHALL RETURN UPON HIS OWN HEAD, AND HIS VIOLENT DEALING SHALL COME DOWN ON HIS OWN CROWN. (KJV)

My inner righteous child held my crown. I had to show myself approved before God to get it back. I had to withstand my trials and tribulations. I prayed that I would make it.

(SUFFERING PERSECUTION AND AFFLICTIONS IN ORDER TO PERSEVERE)

SUFFERING IS WITHOUT DOUBT A HARD TASK TO SWOLLOW AND NOT GIVE UP OR GIVE IN. 2ND TIMOTHY 3 VS 10-13: BUT YOU HAVE CAREFULLY FOLLOWED MY DOCTRINE, MANNER OF LIFE, PURPOSE, FAITH, LONGSUFFERING, LOVE, PERSEVERANCE, PERSECUTIONS, AFFLICTIONS, WHICH HAPPENED TO ME AT ANTIOCH, AT ICONIUM, AT LYSTRA- WHAT PERSECUTIONS I ENDURED. AND OUT OF THEM ALL THE

LORD DELIVERED ME. YES, AND ALL WHO DESIRE TO LIVE GODLY IN CHRIST JESUS WILL SUFFER PERSECUTION. BUT EVIL MEN AND IMPOSTORS WILL GROW WORSE AND WORSE, DECEIVING AND BEING DECEIVED.

You know life is so trickery and you don't know what's going to hit you next. I had been trying to regroup from storm after storm. The enemy was not slacking on his job. He came at me with full force and that force turned deadly. He was not taking any prisoners.

I had just made it out of an affliction of my body. I went through depression after experiencing an accident. I never knew that was really something that can hit you until I could not get a grip on my emotions. It felt like my emotions were on a roller coaster. One minute I was happy, the next I was sad. I was having black outs out of no where; I would be in the store walking and just pass out. I was told to take some medicine; it made me feel like I couldn't get up I was always drowsy. They could not explain to me logically or medically what was wrong. The only thing they could say was because of the head injury that happened in my accident. Tests after tests I was still having black outs and I was in turmoil.

One night I was crying out to God and I told him I would not live my life like that. I refused to take the medicine that kept me numb; I began to go in constant prayer for healing. The medicine they said I would take for the rest of my life I declared it would not hold me bound. I told myself I was not born taking that medicine, so I will not live the rest of my life taking it.

I have not taken the medicine since 2001 and I have not had a black out. I have more good days than bad and I won't complain! Man can say one thing but God has the final say so.

REVELATION 1 VS 8: "I AM THE ALPHA AND THE OMEGA, THE BEGINNING AND THE END," SAYS THE LORD, "WHO IS AND WHO WAS AND WHO IS TO COME, THE ALMIGHTY."

After I made it through that, I thought I would have a breather. I thought I had gone through my worst of worst in 1997-2001. Then I went through the affliction of my body and came out still praising God, despite of!

I was still in the fires of life praying I didn't get burned this time! I told the enemy if he didn't take me down in 1997 then he can't have me now!

In 2000 I had met someone. I wasn't really looking for anyone. I was trying to live my life with some me time. I decided to be with myself and my kids. I had already encountered a crazy man in my life that pulled out a gun on me saying he would kill me because I didn't want to be with him anymore. I wasn't scared because fear wasn't in my nature. By then I knew that God did not create a spirit of fear in me. I told him I would rather die and be in heaven than live in hell with him, in that relationship!

I prayed my way out of that. I told God I would not let another man be with me again unless I am married. After that I just wanted to be by myself with my kids; I didn't want men in and out of their lives, so I kept that part of my life separate from them. The enemy does not care who he uses to destroy you and they don't even know they are being used by him!

Anyway, my daughter (which was about ten or eleven at that time) kept seeing this guy watching us at the tennis court for some time. I would take them there everyday to play. One day he came out and my daughter asked him "why do you keep staring at my mom everyday and not saying anything?" He finally said something. Time went by and we became very close we never moved in with each other but we would see each other almost everyday. I began to fall in love with him. I didn't know what love was but my feelings were different than anything I felt before. I felt he was in love with me but you never can tell with men. I loved the fact that he loved God so much. Even though he was yet in the world he had a special relationship with God; similar to how I did.

To make a long story short; he got into some trouble; usually I would not waste time trying to stay, I always said "if you do the crime you do the time, I am not doing time with you!" This time was different. I stood by him! When he got out we decided to get married. Things were going great. We were in the process of buying a house and planning our wedding. Then things went down hill.

New years eve of 2003 his phone rung and he was in the shower. Of course I answered it and it was a female who hung up at the sound of my voice. I had not had a problem like that with him before. I asked him who was she and of course he lied.

We went to church that night to bring in the New Year. I was trying to keep that off my mind, but I couldn't. The next day I called her and the things she said cut me like a two edged sword. I never knew the heart could feel that kind of pain. I never really loved someone intimately from their soul to their heart before, other than the deep love I have for my children.

I always cared about men for what they could do for me or how they treated me. I was confused about the different kinds of love you have for different people in your life. I always ran when they talked about love to keep from feeling the pain I saw my mother in; when a man was saying he loved her.

I could not separate my feelings concerning love before, because of fear of being in an abusive relationship as my mother was. At that time I wished I had never opened up that kind of love! That pain hurt so badly, I could hardly breathe. I tried for a couple of days to get over it but it would not happen. The pain turned into anger which turned into more anger which caused our break up.

I felt betrayed by the man I really gave my heart to. It wasn't just because he cheated, but because he lied to her about whom I was to him. I was very keen about my worth and he didn't show that he knew this by his actions. She also said she would never leave him alone. I knew I would never trust him again, that alone would eventually ruin our relationship. So I had to make the decision to let go. I didn't know what would hurt more staying with him or letting him go. I don't know how things would have felt to stay but letting go hurt so badly. I knew our relationship would never be the same and I would question his every move. I knew I would not heal with him around me, so I pushed him away.

One thing good he did; was to sign the contract for the house and meet me with the keys. My children and I moved in the house that he and I had picked out. I was in so much pain that the house did not mean anything to me. I was trying to go through this trial so I could heal and not have to revisit that pain ever again.

~~I remember lying in the tub, praying, crying and talking to God and I asked him why did love have to hurt so badly? What did I do wrong to have encountered so much pain? I began to wonder did my love for him get in the way of my love for God; did my love upset God; God is a jealous God! Maybe God took him away from me because my love for him may have altered my steps for my spiritual walk! It felt like I couldn't breath, maybe that love was suffocating the God in me! *Sometimes I wonder do we keep holding on to toxic relationships to keep from feeling the pain of separation from that person or love in our hearts. I wonder do we hold on knowing it's time to let go because the pain is to over bearing to let go, yet we are still hurting when we stay. I just don't know!

I thought love was not pain. I don't know but one thing I did know, it was time for that chapter in my life to end. No matter how hard it was, I had to let him go! So I tried to bury my feelings for him. This wasn't good!

Talking about persecution; my heart was being persecuted for some reason and I didn't know why I already didn't understand that type of pain. I encountered many types of pain in my life's journey but this one, I felt I didn't need it or deserve it. What I did know was I never wanted to feel that pain again!

About three months had gone by and I was still going to work, taking care of my kids trying to heal from the pain. My grandmother was not doing well. She went to the hospital and they wanted to operate, and she told them no. A couple of days afterward I received a call from my sister which was disturbing. She was in Miami with my son's father she informed me; he had gotten killed when he was on his motorcycle. I fell to the floor and just cried. My family, his family, and he and I had a special relationship. After I made the decision not to move there, we never worked out as a couple so we became very close friends. He felt like my big brother at times. My baby son was still with his father and his family in Miami when this happened.

I lost it inside! I could not stop crying my mother was just holding me. I had to make plans to get on a plane to fly to Miami, but I could not function correctly. I was trying but it was hard. I was trying to hold on to every bit of the God in me. I got a flight out two days later. When I arrived there I was still numb. I could not eat, I could not sleep; I was just trying to be strong for my son. Everything was painful to watch. Him lying in the casket; people being dysfunctional with each other just broke my heart. He would not have wanted that. Family meant a lot to him. I told God "I really didn't understand this one seriously!" He was so good to everyone as far as I could see. His heart was of love. Everyone makes mistakes and react in certain ways, because they are still human. I cherished him. He was dear to my heart, no matter what. I was out of sight out of mind! I was not expecting this blow to my heart. I was still recovering and trying to heal from other pain. I was still being broken! I felt God wanted me completely empty! This time it was my heart with my mind.

The funeral and everything was very beautiful. There were so many people paying their respect. There were things going on around me that added more pain. You know what death seems to bring out the greed and the worst of people. That's life; I guess. I had to keep pressing some how. Even with the negative energy coming from soulless people, trying to be a part of destruction, out of greed I had to keep pressing. I could not allow other people's issues to contaminate me any longer. As long as I knew God nothing else mattered, and messiness wouldn't change anything! God always knows what's best, so I asked him to give me the knowledge to do the right things in those situations. No one could ever understand when I said its God's will and not mine in these moments.

I always repeat this saying to myself to help my mind grow and to stay focus:
"GOD GRANT ME THE SERINITY TO ACCEPT THE THINGS I CAN NOT CHANGE, THE COURAGE TO CHANGE THE THINGS I CAN, AND THE WISDOM TO KNOW THE DIFFERENCE."

I had to get back to Atlanta sooner than I wanted to because my grandmother was in the hospital everyone was saying she was giving up. She would not eat or talk. When I got back I was trying to avoid going to the hospital. I was trying to convince myself that she was coming home ok. My aunt called me and said I needed to go to the hospital because the doctors gave my grandmother a couple of days to live. She had refused dialysis at this point. This was the one woman in the world I think loved me more than I loved myself; and showed it! I loved her just as much; we had a special type of bond. She was the one that I would call and just listen to and talk to. She was the one who always had my back and tried to help me see things clearer. She had just become my church buddy all over again. I would pick her up go to church and after church we would go out to eat with the kids. Now she was leaving me, too.

One of my friends finally convinced me to go to the hospital. When I walked through the door she looked over toward me. I lay across her chest and cried until I could not cry any more. I told her I needed her! She told me the only reason she had been holding on was because of us. She had been waiting on me. She said "it was time for her to go that my grandfather was waiting on her." I was trying to ignore that so I feed her, she ate for me. I just wanted her to get better and she just wanted to cross over. I could not take anymore pain; I needed her to stay with me. She had always been strong and to my knowledge she never gave up, even now she wasn't giving up, she was going home to see her King.

The doctors told us that she would not live more than three days after refusing dialysis. I went back to see her, wishing she would get stronger. I sat on her bed because there was no were else to sit; she looked at me and said "get your big behind up I am already on the floor; and smiled at me." She was on a hospital bed that she felt was to low to the floor.

She never held her tongue, that's one thing I can say. She always spoke what was on her mind even to the day she died. Those where the last words I heard her say to me before she went off to see her King.

I was at work the day after visiting her and I got the phone call that my grandmother was gone. I was so devastated I did not know if I was coming or going. I clocked out and walked from my job to my friend's house. This was my friend whose husband passed the same day my son's father passed away. We had been spending a lot of time together trying to help each other through our sorrows.

I walked and cried; I told my grandmother I would be strong I just didn't know how I would keep that promise. I wrote her a poem and read it at her funeral. My family did not think I would make it through, but I did. I told them while tears started running down my face that I told my grandmother last night that I would stand strong and see this through. I know my grandmother went to heaven because that's all she sang about! Even in the mist of all her trials, troubles, afflictions and pain, she held on to the love of God. She always said to me "I will see you tomorrow, God's will." It was no longer God's will for me to see her tomorrow.

In the mist of this, there was a guy that would talk to me just to help me get through the tragedy. I don't know if God sent him to me or was it another trick of the enemy. What ever it was he became my comfort zone from a distance. He was my shoulder to lean on. I was in so much pain I grabbed hold to the most comfortable thing around me and it was him.

I was going through a stage in my life that had I not held on to something I would have been self destructive. I was doing things I didn't want to play apart of my life. I started going out, trying to push the pain away. I started feeling like I had to get away. Something in me was no longer holding on to anything, I was barely breathing.

I went back to work shortly after that trying to continue on, but I could not function. My supervisor called me in the office and was not understanding. I had just lost my son's father and my grandmother Within three weeks of each other. Two very dear people that I held close to my heart. He told me maybe I needed to take some time off. I left and never went back. I could not take it anymore. I didn't know how long it would take to mourn and heal. But what I did know was I was tired of the drama.

I didn't have anymore to give! I didn't care about anything but my sanity, my kids, my heart, my mind and trying to help my sister in the mist of her trial.

My heart felt like a knife was stabbing it daily. I didn't know how God was going to fix my heart, but I asked him to. It was hurting so much and I was falling into a spiritual confusion. A true challenge!

The only thing I felt was right to do was leave. I was trying not to run from anything to face what ever comes against me, but I had to save me. The only thing I felt would save me was to get alone with myself. Within a months time I packed my cloths and moved to another state, far away. I left everything in the house. My family went over and packed it and put everything in storage.

I began a new journey while I was still eating my bread of affliction. The only thing I could think of was God had me. I could not let anyone take me away from being healed by my creator. It was me and God in some weather I had never experienced, in a state I had never lived in before and without anyone really to turn to but God. I was in the mist of long suffering. No one understood why I left and some were not happy with me for leaving, but I had to think about me and the stage my mind was in. If I didn't make a move I would not have been any good for anyone or been able to make it to my next levels with God.

God had to do something in my life that would move me away from everyone so that I could hear only Him. He had to force me out of my comfort zone, into a foreign land. In that land, God had already prepared a table before me even in the mist of my spiritual dark moments, in my unknown spirit. PSALM 23 VS 1-5: THE LORD IS MY SHEPHERD; I SHALL NOT WANT. HE MAKES ME TO LIE DOWN IN GREEN PASTURES; HE LEADS ME BESIDE THE STILL WATERS. HE RESTORES MY SOUL; HE LEADS ME IN THE PATHS OF RIGHTEOUSNESS FOR HIS NAME'S SAKE. YEA THOUGH I WALK THROUGH THE VALLEY OF THE SHADOW OF DEATH, I WILL FEAR NO EVIL; FOR YOU ARE WITH ME; YOUR ROD AND YOUR STAFF, THEY COMFORT ME. YOU PREPARE A TABLE BEFORE ME IN THE PRESENCE OF MY ENEMIES; YOU ANOINT MY HEAD WITH OIL; MY CUP RUNS OVER.
****I WAS SEARCHING FOR SOMETHING THAT WOULD GIVE ME NEW MEANING. I KNEW GOD HAD ANOINTED ME. I NEEDED HIM TO SHOW ME WHO I WAS TIED TO IN THE SPIRIT THAT WOULD HELP ME STAY STRONG EVEN IN MY AFFLICTIONS AND SPIRITUAL GROWTH.

(THE TRUE BLOOD LINE)

The blood came trickling down! During my suffering and afflictions I felt beat down. I felt like I had no one. I often felt like that when I was a teenager, but this was different.

I felt yet again I was dropped in the middle of no where, without a safe guard or life jacket. Without any knowledge of whom I was, all over again. I was lost and confused and did not understand the hand I had been dealt. Inside I felt as if I did not belong in any world, the flesh or spirit.

I had a father that was so smart yet became mentally ill. That disease seemed to flow through his family blood line. I felt like my mother was an alcoholic because she tried to drink her problems away. That disease seemed to flow through her blood line. I didn't feel tracing my flesh or worldly blood line would help me. I was not bound by that anymore.

I was tired of inquiring about it and not getting answers. I think my mom was trying to bury it; which is normal in humans. We try to bury pain. I really don't know but one thing I did know was there was a lot of missing pieces about that part of my life. I never knew why and I never knew what she held inside but what ever it was it was too painful to talk about. Everyone has away of handling their pain and a lot of times the best way is to forget that it happened. At first that's how I began handling my pain until I found out what was missing that could help me release it.

When people feel things are missing inside they began to trace their family tree they wonder who's apart of their blood line. They want to find out where their blood line or genes comes from. It seems as if we began searching for a sense of awareness, something to connect us to power.

But I didn't feel tracing my blood line would define who I am. Things seem so over rated in the genetic field they try and tell you if your parents or their parents had certain genetic defects you would also. That if they carried certain diseases that you or your children would end up with it.

When I looked at my family tree I saw a lot of hustlers and drug dealers that gave in to a life of crime to make money, to feed their family. I found some good relationships, but a lot of bad ones full of deceit and tragedy. I found health problems that left a bad taste in my mouth. I use to think that's all I had to look forward to until I realized something. What truly defined me was connected to that which was fighting to stay alive on the inside of me.

My spiritual blood line is what defined me. It was the very thing that allowed me to be who I am; and what I was made of, and was to become. What I am made of and what defined me was placed in me before birth. That meant my flesh blood line only held merits in the flesh world not the spiritual world.

It was my spiritual genes that would define and determine my true destiny. It is my spiritual genetics that will cover me in my darkest moments. **ROMANS 3 VS 23-25: FOR ALL HAVE SINNED AND FALLEN SHORT OF THE GLORY OF GOD, BEING JUSTIFIED FREELY BY HIS GRACE THROUGH THE REDEMPTION THAT IS IN CHRIST JESUS, WHOM GOD SET FORTH AS A PROPITATION BY HIS BLOOD THROUGH FAITH, TO DEMONSTRATE HIS RIGHTEOUSNESS, BECAUSE IN HIS FORBEARANCE GOD HAD PASSED OVER THE SINS THAT WERE PREVIOUSLY COMMITTED.**

On my spiritual journey and in my last hours of worldly pain and afflictions beyond my understanding, God allowed me to realize something. After I had been stripped of everything the world had thrown at me and in me I searched my soul. When I searched my soul he allowed me to see that my worldly blood line did not hold more power than my spiritual blood line. The true blood line that defined my steps and lead me to my journey had to be traced back to that awesome man who died on the cross. They called Him king and placed a crown of thorns upon His head in mockery of not truly knowing who He was. They took this man named Jesus beat Him near death, commanded Him to carry a cross upon His back up the mountain top. He was given an assistant (Simon) half way there, who would help Him make it the rest of the way. They laid Him on the ground and nailed him by hand and feet to the cross. Then they lifted him up on the cross with blood trickling down and made way for his victory; not knowing that's what they were doing. The enemy thought he was tearing down the character of this awesome man, but little did he know they were preparing Him for His glory and for victory over all. He said; "if I be lifted up, you to shall." By Him I am lifted up even when I am torn down."

I had been given freely a book of life (the bible) to feed my spirit and trace my blood line back to Jesus (God)and back to the cross where my blood line truly began. I had been given something that would lift me up even when I was yet in a world of sin.

It was the blood of my savior that gave me a sense of understanding of my afflictions and adversities that weighed on me. Before He was placed in the womb; God predestined Him to carry out a specific purpose. My destiny is connected to His destination and His life was full of afflictions and adversities. What makes me any better than Jesus that I don't have to eat my bread of affliction and carry my own cross upon my back?

By his birth God showed us love. By his life God showed us gifts and miracles; by the shedding of his blood he saved us and gave us a new life if we walk in the spirit. He allowed all the things that the world subjected us to, to be washed away with the power of his destiny. Jesus allowed me my life back, his blood! **"FOR AS THE FATHER RAISES THE DEAD AND GIVES LIFE TO THEM, EVEN SO THE SON GIVES LIFE TO WHOM HE WILL." JOHN 5 VS 21.**

What ever I did in the flesh, whoever I had become by being obedient to my flesh was washed away by the blood, of my savior. While I lived of the world; I was an enemy of God and did not know it, but by my true blood line I was forgiven. ROMANS 4 VS 8-11: BUT GOD DEMONSTRATES HIS OWN LOVE TOWARD US, IN THAT WHILE WE WERE STILL SINNERS CHRIST DIED FOR US, MUCH MORE THAN HAVING NOW BEEN JUSTIFIED BY HIS BLOOD WE SHALL BE SAVED FROM WRATH THROUGH HIM. FOR IF WHEN WE WERE ENEMIES WE WERE RECONCILED TO GOD THROUGH THE DEATH OF HIS SON, MUCH MORE HAVING BEEN RECONCILED, WE SHALL BE SAVED BY HIS LIFE;AND NOT ONLY THAT BUT WE ALSO REJOICE IN GOD THROUGH WHOM WE HAVE NOW RECEIVED THE RECONCILIATION.

My blood line was full of mercy. I dug deep within to trace my true blood line. I found the blood that cried out for me, the blood that saved me and set me free. This blood reconciled my relationship with God. I was no longer an enemy to the one whom created and predestined me. I was His heir. The blood connected me back to my creator which released all those gifts and talents, back to its rightful owner; me and God! That which was in bondage was restored and I was redeemed.

ROMANS 8 VS 23: NOT ONLY THAT, BUT WE ALSO WHO HAVE THE FIRST FRUITS OF THE SPIRITS, EVEN WE OURSELVES GROAN WITHIN OURSELVES, EAGERLY WAITING FOR THE ADOPTION, THE REDEMPTION OF OUR BODY. Redemption was one of the strongest recoveries that my soul encountered when I came face to face with who I use to be. I could not have ever imagined that my walk in life would hold some similar steps as my savior's did, once I stepped back into the will of God. Through the knowledge and understanding of his life and death I found in me a new life full of understanding and faith.

This blood is the blood that will never lose its power. This blood saves us even as we walked in sin. This blood was and is the one blood line I was proud to trace back. I gained a spiritual awareness that allowed me to find out that the true blood line is the blood that covered and kept me, even when I yet walked in darkness.

So much strength this man (the one with my true blood line) had even when things were weighed upon His back. He pushed and pressed His way through even with knowledge that His time had come. He never complained or let things faze him. He healed those that were sick, raised the dead, and allowed the blind to see. He saw things before they happened and still walked to His destiny. These are the genetic outputs that I want in me.

This man laid down His life even for His enemies and bled so that everyone who chose Him could be free. This is the blood that captivated me. This blood line made me proud to be a child of God, pressing to the kingdom. By the blood He bled He let my eyes see, God held the keys to life and my destiny.

Then I found the greatest love of them all resting deep down underneath the blood that flowed in me, God. This blood line is the one blood line that was a product of pure love! It connects us to one body that makes up many members yet we treat each others like enemies. It's not what we look like on the outside it's what flows from us, if either one of us is cut or hurt. **Blood!**

1ST CORINTHIANS 12 VS 12 AND 18-27: FOR AS THE BODY IS ONE AND HAS MANY MEMBERS, BUT ALL THE MEMBERS OF THAT ONE BODY, BEING MANY, ARE ONE BODY, SO ALSO IS CHRIST. VS 18-27: BUT NOW GOD HAS SET THE MEMBERS, EACH ONE OF THEM, IN THE BODY JUST AS HE PLEASED. AND IF THEY WERE ALL ONE MEMBER, WHERE WOULD THE BODY BE? AND THE EYE CANNOT SAY TO THE HAND, "I HAVE NO NEED OF YOU"; NOR AGAIN THE HEAD TO THE FEET, "I HAVE NO NEED OF YOU." NO, MUCH RATHER, THOSE MEMBERS OF THE BODY WHICH SEEM TO BE WEAKER ARE NECESSARY. AND THOSE MEMBERS OF THE BODY WHICH WE THINK TO BE LESS HONORABLE, ON THESE WE BESTOW GREATER HONOR; AND OUR UNPRESENTABLE PARTS HAVE GREATER MODESTY, BUT OUR PRESENTABLE PARTS HAVE NO NEED. BUT GOD COMPOSED THE BODY, HAVING GIVEN GREATER HONOR TO THAT PART WHICH LACKS IT, THAT THERE SHOULD BE NO SCHISM IN THE BODY, BUT THAT THE MEMBERS SHOULD HAVE THE SAME CARE FOR ONE ANOTHER. AND IF ONE MEMBER SUFFERS, ALL THE MEMBERS SUFFER WITH IT; OR IF ONE MEMBER IS HONORED, ALL THE MEMBERS REJOICE WITH IT. NOW YOU ARE THE BODY OF CHRIST, AND MEMBERS INDIVIDUALLY.

LISTEN~ Can you trace your worldly blood line back to such an awesome blood line? Can your blood line wash away all your sins and remember them no more? Can your blood line release gifts to you beyond worldly mysteries? Does your blood line set you free or does it bound you to life's tragedies? Does your blood line create in you a clean heart? Can your blood line heal your body of all diseases if you just believe it?

It was the blood that trickled down which turned my life around! When Babylon fell down from upon me the blood set my soul free and allowed me to rise from captivity. It was the blood! My real blood line! My blood line that fills voids and helps me understand who I am! The blood line that connects me yet makes me different from any other man! The blood line that will allow me to see what really matters is what dwells inside of me! I am who I am in darkness and out of darkness! Darkness and light is no different if he rests inside me. This was the blood line that helped me survive storm after storm, even when I was torn between two worlds. Ashes to ashes and dust to dust I was made, but it was this blood line in which I was saved! **MY BLOOD LINE! THE TRUE BLOOD LINE!**

CHAPTER SIX

UNDERSTANDING THE VALUE OF X (U-X)

X= ANYTHING THAT ONCE WAS AND IS TRYING TO HOLD ON AND KEEP YOU ENTANGLED IN ITS TRAPS. ***STEP INTO THE KNOWLEDGE OF YOUR LIFE'S TIME FRAME BY GAINING UNDERSTANDING OF YOUR LIFE'S GUIDE LINE. BEFORE YOU AWAKEN X FIGURE OUT WHAT IS THE PURPOSE FOR IT AND THEN WALK IT OUT!!

(UNDER RECONSTRUCTION)

Understand me; I am giving you no excuses. My behavior may not seem productive to you, but I'm fighting through years of mental abuse. I have stumbled and fell then taken over by hell. I rose up high with tears burning my eyes. I looked to the world for help when I couldn't help myself and it denied me. What my eyes saw damaged my soul and caused hell to shift into over load. So excuse me if you don't like what you see or don't understand what's in me. But this is what happens when you're raised by the streets, or your mind is left in captivity.

You say my environment does not justify my mean, but if you did a trading places how would you escape the world's enemy? The world is filled with many faces that hide behind devastation. I was under reconstruction you see and that mess had to come out of me.

I was predestined before my spirit took form in the womb. The enemy, he peeked in and saw who I was then sent out his soldiers to destroy me. The attack was deadly, yet I survived. The thousand deaths I died, yet it kept my soul alive. After those many trials and obstacles I pressed my way through, leaving holes inside of me. I was underestimating the enemy's plan, thinking I was my own man. I was playing the devil's advocate; doing his job until everything fell apart. I had to look within and find out who God really was behind the iron wall.

The yellow tape had to go up to warn those: you may not like what you see, but it was God rising up in me as my flesh died to the streets. There were things that weren't of him that had to know its place, so it had to step down to be erased. I had to be covered with the blood and turn my heart into love, so that I could begin my new journey. A big whole was left inside of me, where the world had buried my soul beneath. So excuse me if you don't like what you see, but my master is rising up in me.

Due to my reconstruction I may not seem to be myself but soon I will become a new woman of true wealth. So maybe you don't like what you see because you thought I did not have a chance to become all God placed in me, before the world snatched me into captivity. I had to go under reconstruction and yes you had to go, even though I loved you and thought I needed you near. God whispered something else in my ear. It was time for my flesh to disappear! It could no longer rule over my thoughts or control the paths in which I would walk. My steps have been ordered from the man above so my spirit must transcend and take form. I have been redeemed by the blood. My soul shall raise above my physical genes and over ride anything that binds me to the streets of pain and misery. I rose up high; loosen the shackles that bounded me by the things this world believed to be. Then my inner man began to be set free.

2ND CORITHIANS 4 VS 16-18: THEREFORE WE DO NOT LOSE HEART. EVEN THOUGH OUR OUTWARD MAN IS PERISHING, YET THE INWARD MAN IS BEING RENEWED DAY BY DAY. FOR OUR LIGHT AFFLICTION, WHICH IS BUT FOR A MOMENT, IS WORKING FOR US A FAR MORE EXCEEDING AND ETERNAL WEIGHT OF GLORY, WHILE WE DO NOT LOOK AT THE THINGS WIIICII ARE SEE, BUT AT THE THINGS WHICH ARE NOT SEEN. FOR THE THINGS WHICH ARE SEEN ARE TEMPORARY, BUT THE THINGS WHICH ARE NOT SEEN ARE ETERNAL.

(VICTIMS INTO VICTORY)

2ND CORINTHIANS 4 VS 10-15: ALWAYS CARRYING ABOUT IN THE BODY THE DYING OF THE LORD JESUS, THAT THE LIFE OF JESUS ALSO MAY BE MANIFESTED IN OUR BODY. FOR WE WHO LIVE ARE ALWAYS DELIVERED TO DEATH FOR JESUS SAKE, THAT THE LIFE OF JESUS ALSO MAY BE MANIFESTED IN OUR MORTAL FLESH. SO THEN DEATH IS WORKING IN US, BUT LIFE IN YOU. AND SINCE WE HAVE THE SAME SPIRIT OF FAITH, ACCORDING TO WHAT IS WRITTEN, "I BELIEVE AND THEREFORE SPEAK, KNOWING THAT HE WHO ROSE UP THE LORD JESUS WILL ALSO RAISE US UP WITH JESUS, AND WILL PRESENT US WITH YOU. FOR ALL THINGS ARE FOR YOUR SAKES, THAT GRACE, HAVING SPREAD THROUGH THE MANY, MAY CAUSE THANKSGIVING TO ABOUND TO THE GLORY OF GOD.

When I realized whom I was connected to in my true blood line I began to see more clearly how vicious the enemy was, but victory was God's love! Though I had to walk that walk God brought me out. In order to find myself I had to die to myself. I might have thought a bad hand I was dealt, until I visualized how Jesus may have wept for me.

His cross became my cross and only at the cross could my true life be brought about. I came to realize that even though Jesus died on the cross he had to carry it first. He carried it on his back up to the top of the mountain. My walk in the world, my life in the world was me carrying my cross. The pain, the misery and the streets I carried them on my back. I carried it up mountains and through valleys. It weighed my body down and my heart begins to feel the sword cutting deep within, until it drained all my tears.

I had to die to this world and press toward the hill. My spirit gained strength to rise within my tears. At that point my destiny began to be revealed on top of those mountains and hills that I climbed in my mind.

In the mist of all the torture, all the abuse, all the starvation, and all the tormenting my destiny had found me. Though I had to die to the world I didn't have to shed blood, because my savior had already bled for me. By his blood I had already gained victory.

1ST CORINTHIANS 15 VS 50-57: NOW THIS I SAY, BRETHREN THAT FLESH AND BLOOD CANNOT INHERIT THE KINGDOM OF GOD; NOR DOES CORRUPTION INHERIT INCORRUPTION. BEHOLD, I TELL YOU A MYSTERY; WE SHALL NOT ALL SLEEP, BUT WE SHALL ALL BE CHANGED- IN A MOMENT, IN THE TWINKLING OF AN EYE, AT THE LAST TRUMPET. FOR THE TRUMPET WILL SOUND, AND THE DEAD WILL BE RAISED INCORRUPTIBLE, AND WE SHALL BE CHANGED. FOR THIS CORRUPTIBLE MUST PUT ON INCORUPTION, AND THIS MORTAL MUST PUT ON IMMORTALITY. SO WHEN THIS CORRUPTIBLE HAS PUT ON INCORRUPTION, AND THIS MORTAL HAS PUT ON IMMORTALITY, THEN SHALL BE BROUGHT TO PASS THE SAYING THAT IS WRITTEN: "DEATH, WHERE IS YOUR STING? O HADES, WHERE IS YOUR VICTORY?" THE STING OF DEATH IS SIN, AND THE STRENGTH OF SIN IS THE LAW. BUT THANKS BE TO GOD, WHO GIVES US THE VICTORY THROUGH OUR LORD JESUS CHRIST.

We become our own victims and become bound by our own flesh to think thoughts that keep us in chains. We fight against our own flesh and blood because we don't understand we are not in control. I began to think that our true victim is the God in us, not who we are in the world. Things may come our way, this is not to tear us down but to build us up and bring out the real man that holds our life's plan.

Don't spend so much time being a victim or allowing yourself to become a victim. That's what the enemy wants so the world can keep kicking you down. You have to let the world know that even as they kick you're still rising. When the world talks down you, you are growing. You will not stand as a victim to please anyone; you will become victorious, for He is in you!

We lose who we are in being a victim and end up not finding out whom or what we were to become; which is victorious! Every hill and every valley low comes to show us and teach us how to grow! So that we can become victorious over our struggles! The victim is no more.

(WHEN DOES TRUE WISDOM STEP IN?)

ECCLESIASTES 3vs 1: TO EVERYTHING THERE IS A SEASON, A TIME FOR EVERY PURPOSE UNDER HEAVEN:

Wisdom is the manifestation of knowledge when you find it, you find life! During my life span I had been giving my body, and sacrificing more of my soul. I didn't know at the time, but the enemy did. I wasn't really putting up a fight because I felt I was doing something with my life. We are always saying I! I! I! I! I figured out that my greatest enemy was myself living in pain, and my greatest successor was my enemy.

The greatest fight in the world I encountered was the fight I had within myself when the world spit me out. The greatest fight you will ever have is the fight you will have with yourself, when the world is finished with you and you can't go any further in the world, without being connected to your creator.

When you have been chewed up and spit back out. When you've been devoured and striped of everything you were before birth. When you've been abused and used up. When you've been sucked into the streets with no help: to find your way. When your mind has been feed trash over and over by the ones who say they love you. When your innocence has been taken by someone unknown and known what do you feel? When your eyes have seen street deaths and people put in trunks. When one side of your family is dysfunctional and alcoholics on the other side! When you've given all of yourself and you have nothing else to give. When your heart is made of stone and you look life in the face and see nothing left.

When pain has become your best friend and misery stepped right in. When you can't trust anyone or recognize the good in anyone. When you have lost everything that meant anything to you. When you have nothing, nothing to hold on to, nothing you feel, nothing seems to be there; you can't see it but that's when the mind becomes free to understand your blessings are in your struggles, in your pain, in your heart aches and in his name (Jesus). When you have gotten to a place where the fight is greater than your strength and your mind just can't comprehend; that's when true wisdom begins.

ECCLESIASTES 7 VS11-14: WISDOM IS GOOD WITH AN INHERITANCE, AND PROFITABLE TO THOSE WHO SEE THE SUN. FOR WISDOM IS A DEFENSE AS MONEY IS A DEFENSE, BUT THE EXCELLENCE OF KNOWLEDGE IS THAT WISDOM GIVES LIFE TO THOSE WHO HAVE IT. CONSIDER THE WORK OF GOD; FOR WHO CAN MAKE STRAIGHT WHAT HE HAS MADE CROOKED? IN THE DAY OF PROSPERITY BE JOYFUL, BUT IN THE DAY OF ADVERSITY CONSIDER: SURELY GOD HAS APPOINTED THE ONE AS WELL AS THE OTHER, SO THAT MAN CAN FIND OUT NOTHING THAT WILL COME AFTER HIM.

In the mist of all of our afflictions and adversities we are formed in the flesh not because we were weak, but because we must be made strong in the spirit, so that our soul can get to its destiny.

People always try to give their opinion to why we are the way we are. The world tries to say that our environment does not create our worldly being; I am a living testimony that my environment created who I had become in the world and in my flesh. My mind was so confused that it led me to believe I couldn't be anything more. Yet my spirit allowed me to see beyond what the world showed me. My spirit allowed me to rise above the rapture of the enemy to conquer what waits for me; my destiny!

*Thought from my mind: if the world strips you to nothing outward and your mind has been governed to think a certain way inward you leave an imprint in your mind to manifest that which you have dwelled on. What's in your mind will soon manifest one way or another. Either negative or positive will unfold it depends on which one you give the most power and energy to. Distraction is placed there to break you down and take your mind off important things like wisdom, knowledge, and faith.

The world is a heart breaker and a soul shaker. If you can't see past those iron walls you will step into one of life's biggest falls. When I fell I fell hard. I fell to nothing but God, my kids and I; the moment I fell, my creator picked me up. At that moment my true life began. I carried my own cross through my worldly struggles, all the way into my spiritual awareness. I felt myself becoming one of God's true warriors. I looked beaten and weak on the outside, on the inside I was being built up and was coming alive. Wisdom stepped in me and began to set my mind free. It felt like the incredible hulk was coming forth; in the spiritual realm because as my soul rose things just seemed to fall off of me and my spirit grew bolder and bigger.

Stepping from my fall my heart seemed to be torn yet being built up. The heart is an awesome vessel. God understands the heart more than anyone in this world he developed its purpose. He is the only one that can heal it and comfort it! It's a part of the body that holds feelings, emotions, love, and life. It is a vessel that keeps life going. Some things we can't live without; the heart is one of them. When we don't understand why so much pain; wisdom shows up and like God, shows out!

Pain begets pain, love begets love. When souls connect they begin to fill holes that were dug in the mist of loses and falls. Sometimes we allow other souls in to our bodies that don't belong there. Once in, old wounds are opened causing more pain to beget the new pain. After I learned to let go my true wisdom showed up. It awakened my mind to see life as it unfolded from pain to love. I had to learn to let go! I learned it was not my understanding that would get me there; it was me trusting God no matter what that would eventually take me to higher levels.

Wisdom was found as I came back up from those great falls in my life in the heart of my soul.

X =THE POWER OF GOD'S TIME LINE IN
*****LIFE*****

X plays a factor in everything connected to life. If you do not develop a sense of awareness which connects you to the facts of life you begin to enter and exit into wrong doors. We end up with a lot of x things instead of current thoughts, not knowing what time it is. Those x things cause you to carry around extra baggage inside, which harms your spiritual development and self awareness. Without standing on faith you fall into a place of despair. **HEBREWS 11 VS 3: BY FAITH WE UNDERSTAND THAT THE WORLDS WERE FRAMED BY THE WORD OF GOD, SO THAT THE THINGS WHICH ARE SEEN WERE NOT MADE OF THINGS WHICH ARE VISIBLE.**

We forget there is a time for everything in our life. This leads us to become spiritually bankrupt because we are leading ourselves from past things (x things) instead of being lead by him that holds our now and future. **ECCLESIASTES 3 VS 2-4: A TIME TO BE BORN, AND A TIME TO DIE; A TIME TO PLANT, AND A TIME TO PLUCK WHAT IS PLANTED; A TIME TO KILL, AND A TIME TO HEAL; A TIME TO BREAK DOWN, AND A TIME TO BUILD UP; A TIME TO WEEP, AND A TIME TO LAUGH; A TIME TO MOURN A TIME TO DANCE;** I began thinking how awesome and mysterious our creator is. It took Him seven days to create heaven, earth, and then He even rested.

I really feel inside that God used seven years in the time frame for my life. In those seven year increments He was building a stronger and wiser warrior.

The first seven years of my life from birth to seven God walked with me, talked with me and created His life in me. I believe He installed all the equipment I would need to withstand the wilderness: knowledge, power, His words, love, peace, joy and wisdom. He allowed me to be born with money. He gave me a praying grandmother and mother. I was very intelligent. I knew a lot for my age.

Then the enemy stepped in. It took satan (the enemy) seven years to intrude on my spirit to try and devour my soul. From the age eight to fifteen the enemy tormented me. he sent pain to kill my spirit and bury my soul. he commanded another man's pain to take my joy hostage. he released chaos to disturb my peace. he gave me ammunition to use my knowledge and so called wisdom for worldly gain. I became upset that my mother named me **UGANDA.** Kids used that as a way to tear me down for the enemy. It became the ammunition they used to cause me to become confused about my identity. It became another source that fed energy to my anger that caused more fights. I didn't know that my name was connected to what was inside of me. I didn't know the strength it possessed the power it held!

The next seven years from age sixteen to twenty-three I felt God took his arms from me, as He did job. During that time I wandered in the world full of sin. I was lukewarm one minute and cold the other. I knew about God, but I let the world get the best of me. Those seven years demonstrated my spirit being stripped of its heir and righteousness, which took away the power it, was given at birth. It represented the wilderness and the flesh being my master. **GALATIANS 4VS 3- 7: EVEN SO WE, WHEN WE WERE CHILDREN WERE IN BONDAGE UNDER THE ELEMENTS OF THE WORLD. BUT WHEN THE FULLNESS OF THE TIME HAD COME, GOD SENT FORTH HIS SON, BORN OF A WOMAN, BORN UNDER THE LAW, TO REDEEM THOSE WHO WERE UNDER THE LAW, THAT WE MIGHT RECEIVE THE ADOPTION AS SONS. AND BECAUSE YOU ARE SONS, GOD HAS SENT FORTH THE SPIRIT OF HIS SON INTO YOUR HEARTS, CRYING OUT, "ABBA, FATHER!" THEREFORE YOU ARE NO LONGER A SLAVE BUT A SON AND IF A SON, THE HEIR OF GOD THROUGH CHRIST.**

The next seven years of my life from age twenty-four to thirty one I started letting go! I started studying my creator to find out what was going on with my life. I began to release things and I started dying within. It is written that you should seek yee first the kingdom of God and all else will be given. I begin to realize that my steps had been ordered. That even though I did not understand why so much pain, it was the pain that enlightened me and led me to a place where I would find peace. In this place my mother became my best friend, understanding I am who I am.

During this period of my life I thought I was losing my mind. I began to encounter things in my life that would cause man to separate themselves from the love of God, but I had already decided that I was not going back only forward. The enemy does not care who he uses or what tricks he uses to try and take you down. I was told if he is not messing with you he is not worried about who you are, because you're already entangled in his web. I had begun to look at life from an inner view, and not an outer view. The way God works is a mystery beyond awesomeness to me.

Even though I felt like I was losing my mind I realized this time line was set up as one of God's greatest master plans ever put together. Some people my age are going through things I have already conquered. Some people older than me are still walking in the wilderness trying to find their way out of darkness. Not to say anything is wrong with that because everyone serves a specific purpose at their specific time of their life.

He has allowed me to figure things out. He has given me gifts allowing, me to see and hear beyond what eyes and ears can see or hear. "Eyes have not seen and ears have not heard."

If you allow your spirit to awaken you step into a place of restoration and redemption. Which allows you to begin to understand that your paths where ordered by choices. That your walk begins each time you wake up and step into a new day. In order to become destiny, you must let go and stand strong through anything that is thrown at you.

YOU ARE THE PRODUCT OF YOUR SELFLESSNESS! DENY SELF! KNOW THYSELF! TO THYSELF BE TRUE! I became the product of my selflessness! Once you are delivered from self and let spirit take over a new birth in you takes place. Look into your life and figure out your time line. Know your valleys and your mountains. Figure out what you did in the valleys and what God did to get you back to the mountain tops. Find out when you were most productive, and where your mind frame and spirit was. Become your own challenge to get to every finish line your heart desires by knowing your place.

Hold on to every piece of the things you are asking for or working toward. No matter what is falling down around you, or what tricks the enemy has brought up against you.

If you stand fast in the word; that which you have faith in or that which your heart desires, your life's time line will soon fall in place. That which your creator gave to you before birth you shall receive. Then you find out that X reveals your walks in the wilderness, in the flesh, in the world, and then in the spirit. It also reveals how long you stay in each. It never matters why or how you got to a place only what you do in them and how you come out of them.

If you don't walk in the wilderness how will you get to the place where your soul is free? Your spirit can gain the strength to rise and step into its destiny. It can become a source of energy that gives light unto this world, even as you stand in the wilderness of darkness.

Real talk: In the Bible's book Exodus there is a man name Moses. He led the people of Israel out of Egypt. When God allowed them to leave he took them through the wilderness. He did that so in fear they would not turn back to where they were once captive. They didn't understand why he took them through the wilderness. But God knew, because that's the way He needed them to go; He needed to show them He was still God and He can bring them out of the wilderness from the hands of their enemy. They came upon the red sea. God told Moses to stretch out his rod. It parted the Red Sea. As you read in **Exodus 14,** you will find life lessons and obstacles taking place. There is one thing that stood out to me. It was repeated several times: the children of Israel in the mist of the Red Sea crossed on dry land.

They were escaping that which once had them captive. They were walking through the wilderness, came upon the Red Sea, which was parted for them to walk across on dry land. The land is dry, yet they are walking through a sea with water on both sides of them. I believe God made known that it was dry land, for me to understand that when you come through the wilderness anything that was your past will remain in the past or drown in the sea behind you. Though I may go through storms (rain and wind) and walk through the unknown, He will allow the land I tread my feet to stay dry so that nothing from my past will be tracked into my future, my newness; my enlarged territory; my land of milk and honey.

THINGS TO PONDER ABOUT:

Can we ever become that which we were created to become without painful life experiences? Who would you be or have become if you didn't know who you were in the spirit or flesh? If you never walked in the wilderness how would you gain strength to surpass your past? Strength to hold on when you have nothing left; strength to figure out that what is in you is not to tear you down, but to lead you to your true crown. People proclaim having voids in their life because of lost, never having, a bad child hood, one parent homes, and their environment along with many other circumstances. Those things play a great part in which we become, but it does not say who we are. We were made from dust and the breath of God. Wind alone will cause dust to scatter if it is not held together by the power of our creator. The battles, the pain, the heart aches and the bumpy roads of life are the wind that blows against us and causes us to crumble. The breath of God is the power that keeps us together. If we separate ourselves from Him we are scattered amongst the deadness of life, fighting battles that are not ours which cause voids in every part of our life; the heart, soul, mind, and relationships.

The void that lies in lost souls and dead spirits is not due to lost, not having, and any other tragedy or pain. Our voids come when we don't know the strength in the breath that was breathed in us. Our purpose is connected to our creator. If we are not connected to the source that fills voids, then we hold on to those things that were not meant to continue or play apart in our life. We use these things as a clutch or something that becomes our excuse when we fail. We have to stop feeling sorry for ourselves and do something about it.

We don't need an excuse. God knew us before we knew ourselves. He knew the mistakes and bad decisions we would make. He knew that we would fall and yet he gave us the strength to get back up. He knew that we would have some good days and some bad days. He knew we would have hills to climb. That's what Jesus died for. When we live in the spirit we understand our walk was predestined to create a perfect vessel that God needs for His perfect body. Once we realize that we are who we are, that man does not define us, it's coming out of our valley lows that shows us we are growing and that our pain and our struggles is not us it's just apart of creating who we were predestined to be.

Have you ever thought that when God breathed in us that He left apart of Him to take form and manifest an awesome being? We have to learn we are a powerful force that can create a whole world if we tap into what lies within us. We are free spirits that have been given the knowledge of this divine universe. That knowledge lies in the mind. We where created with a mind, body, and soul: spirit, soul, body. It all is built up in threes like the Father, Son, and Holy Spirit. Powerful combinations!

CHAPTER SEVEN

YESTERDAY'S FIGHTING HAS TO STOP, THEN YOU CAN BE TRULY FREE! (Y-Z)

WARRIORS PLEASE STAND UP FOR THIS BATTLE IS NOT YOURS! YESTERDAY'S FIGHTING CAUSED THE ENEMY'S SHADOW TO REAP WAR WITH THE INNER MAN. THE INNER MAN BECAME MY ENEMY BRINGING FORTH GREAT WARS. BUT THE WAR BROUGHT DEVASTATING BATTLES WHICH RELEASED A TRUE WORRIER!

YOU NEED TO STOP FIGHTING WITH SELF CAUSE IT'S TIME TO WRESTLE WITH GOD

Your eyes have not seen nor have your ears heard what happens when you get alone with yourself and God. The inner fighting must stop. You have to stop fighting yourself, your past, your today, and your own mind, and wrestle with someone that holds your future. One day you will figure out as I did that you have two major choices you will either stay shackled in bondage to your past or you will step out of self and find your destiny. It is time to figure out who you are spiritually so that your worldly fights won't live as a constant battle in your mind.

There is a reason why you need alone time in order to move beyond your circumstances, that's God time with you. That time places you in a position where you and your master can be face to face in the spirit.

If you do not realize the things that are weighing you down are the very things that were only placed there to build you up and make you stronger you become lost fighting fights that hold no reward. You will begin to tumble into a place of desire, if you don't allow your inner being to stop fighting with the world (the enemy).

Just imagine being able to unzip the past and your new man steps out and all the old things drop off and are remembered no more. I realized the reason I needed my worldly lost was to get me to my spiritual destiny. Everything I accomplished was a part of my release. Once I begin to see wonders and mysteries beyond recognition I knew I was moving to new levels. Everything I thought was lost was and is being restored daily. The one thing that gave me comfort, knew God was back speaking to me and I could hear Him more and more each day. He has released to me gifts that the world can't take away. He blessed me with a new mind! Thank God he gives many chances! Thank God he gave me the strength that allowed me to be willing to lay down my life, leave everything and body to Him and fight for what was mine!

GENESIS 32 VS 22-28: AND HE AROSE THAT NIGHT AND TOOK HIS TWO WIVES, HIS TWO FEMALE SERVANTS, AND HIS ELEVEN SONS, AND CROSSED OVER THE FORD OF JABBOK. HE TOOK THEM, SENT THEM OVER THE BROOK, AND SENT OVER WHAT HE HAD. THEN JACOB WAS LEFT ALONE; AND AN ANGEL OF GOD WRESTLED WITH HIM UNTIL THE BREAKING OF DAY. NOW WHEN HE SAW THAT HE DID NOT PREVAIL AGAINST JACOB, HE TOUCHED THE SOCKET OF HIS HIP; AND THE SOCKET OF JACOB'S HIP WAS OUT OF JOINT AS HE WRESTLED WITH HIM. AND HE SAID, "LET ME GO, FOR THE DAY BREAKS." BUT JACOB SAID, "I WILL NOT LET YOU GO UNLESS YOU BLESS ME!" SO THE ANGEL OF GOD SAID TO HIM, "WHAT IS YOUR NAME?" HE SAID, "JACOB" AND HE SAID, "YOUR NAME SHALL NO LONGER BE CALLED JACOB, BUT ISRAEL; FOR YOU HAVE STRUGGLED WITH GOD AND WITH MEN, AND HAVE PREVAILED."

One day you will realize that what's holding you back, crowding your thoughts, entangling your mind, hindering your growth, and taken up valuable space in your life needs to go or you will continue to live in darkness; lost and confused with your peace held up in chains along with your inner man. In order to find peace you have to get back to the man that holds peace in his hands. We have to search for a place to be with just ourselves and God. A lot of times we have things around use that keeps us from hearing from our creator. Those things were placed there by the enemy to distract us from hearing our creator's voice. It's about you, your inner man and God. **PSALMS 62 VS 1: TRULY MY SOUL SILENTLY WAITS FOR GOD; FROM HIM COMES MY SALVATION.**

When I was growing up I had that noise from the iron fist constantly playing in my inner ear and my inner mind. Those fights caused me to begin fighting with myself and others. The fight with myself caused inner wars that I was not equipped to fight. The enemy had blinded me from seeing my birth rights. I had allowed him to take my soul hostage by letting my flesh war with my spirit.

I began to realize I had to allow yesterday's fighting to stay in yesterday. Once I did that I was able to step into my today's and prepare for my tomorrows. When all was said and done I realized that I would have never become truly free until yesterday was stripped from me.

We try to hold on to yesterday kicking and screaming because for one we need something to define us and give us a sense of security and yesterday gives us a sense of whom we think we are. Secondly we fear the unknown. We can't understand that our yesterday holds us in yesterday, and will not allow us into our today. We try to live in two worlds and deprive ourselves of the wholeness of today! If we continue to imprison ourselves and allow our minds to be bound by yesterday's mess we stay trapped in the snares of the enemy, where we never become free!

A piece of paper may say our bodies are free but where our spirits lies tells us if our mind is free. Once we free our minds the rest follows. It doesn't matter if our body is chained in shackles, if our mind is resting in the breast plate of righteousness man (the world) can't control us or our destiny; even when they think they are.

The greatest fight I ever had was with myself. One day you will realize the greatest fight you will ever have is within you. The greatest reward I found was knowing that God had prevailed in the fight against man, me and the angel of God that had come upon me. With God I stood when I could not stand anymore. With hell all around I was still was holding on to God, telling Him I was not going to let go until He blessed me. I didn't look back no matter how things felt! And I finally became free.

The only way I was able to accomplish this was letting go! Letting go of all the things around me that caused my soul to suffer many afflictions! Then I went to a place where it would be just me and God. My heart felt as if a knife was in it, my mind was in turmoil, so I let everything go; just long enough to find the God in me and allow Him to breath! But oh how glad I am that I did because now my mind is free therefore so is my body.

I knew the only way the fighting in my mind, life, and with God would stop was to surrender my life to God. I had to throw in the towel. Put my hands up and get face to face with my master. I thought I had emptied all the things that caused me to separate myself from the love of God. I might have, but I felt as if everything that imprisoned my mind was drowning me. No one would understand unless they were walking in my shoes.

They could not understand because it was going on in the inside of me and not the outside. They could not feel my pain, so they could not help me through it.

There was a powerful battle being held within. The enemy did not want the God in me to rise. My shoes spiritually are some big shoes to fill. Not everyone can stand through those storms without losing their mind.

The fight is not physical it's always mental (in your mind). That's why people play with your mind, because they know it will cause you to react physically. If you master your mind people will not be able to contaminate your thoughts. They will not be able to cause you to step out of your Godly self. If you don't know by now, one day soon you will. That's why people judge by the outer appearance, they allow their flesh to rule over their mind.

A great man (my grandfather) told me "if you kill the head (the mind) the body will fall." If you are trying to fight with flesh you will never take the enemy down. The enemy is in your mind trying to kill the body. I realized that some things you have to let go and roll down your back, because it's trying to keep your mind in bondage.

******* It's time to break free! It's time in your life to send everything away. Let everything go that will keep you out of the love and will of God. Be alone, at least until you find yourself, and set your mind free. I told myself; if I'm going to walk through hell (the fighting, the streets, the pain, the misery, and the darkness) I might as well bring back the keys to open up heaven on earth for me now. If you have walked through the life of hell you might as well bring back the keys for your life and open up your destiny!

We are heirs to the throne! We are royalty. We must begin to walk like we are, talk like we are, and live like we are. We must become truly free by freeing the one thing the enemy has been trying to take down and take control of; our mind, the word in us, our soul! The world didn't give it to you and all though it tried to take it, it can't! I was named a country at birth. I was a whole country inside before birth and now I am walking with the strength of a whole country to gain my crown and conquer my destiny!

**How awesome was and is God, that He used my mom at my birth to name me a whole country: <u>UGANDA!</u> I didn't have to be renamed after wrestling with the angels of God. He had already made me whole! The enemy wanted to take me down because God created in me the strength of a whole country. The enemy was scared that I would find strength to bring him down! Every time I woke up he was upset and was trying to kill me. Now I know why!!!!! I am who I am! Even in and apart from darkness! Just as you are who you are! A force to be reckoned with!!! Especially if you are connected with the right one! <u>God!!!</u> <u>With Him you can conquer anything!!!!</u>

What's your new name or is it the same, just stronger in knowing who you are? Now you are at the point where you can begin to conquer the world in you, with your mind free to allow God to take control of what's trying to take control of you! God will surely take him down. Let him know God is in control!

(ZION IS WAITING FOR YOU!)

Zion is one of the hills on which Jerusalem stood. It now applies to the temple, the whole of Jerusalem, its people as a community whose destiny depends on God. Zion also is a symbol of <u>heaven</u>.

PSALMS 50 VS 1-5: THE MIGHTY ONE, GOD THE LORD, HAS SPOKEN AND CALLED THE EARTH FROM THE RISING OF THE SUN TO IT'S GOING DOWN. OUT OF ZION, THE PERFECTION OF BEAUTY, GOD WILL SHINE FORTH. OUR GOD SHALL COME, AND SHALL NOT HAVE DEEP SILENT; A FIRE SHALL DEVOUR BEFORE HIM, AND IT SHALL BE VERY TEMPESTUOUS ALL AROUND HIM. HE SHALL CALL TO THE HEAVENS FROM ABOVE, AND TO THE EARTH, THAT HE MAY JUDGE HIS PEOPLE: "GATHER MY SAINTS TOGETHER TO ME, THOSE WHO HAVE MADE A COVENANT WITH ME BY SACRIFICE". Never under estimate the greatness that is being suppressed deep down within you. For we hold valuable resources in our mind and soul. That's why the enemy declares war on those whom God has called. The enemy wants our birth rights. He wants to take from us that which God breathed in us and spoke over our lives. GENESIS 2 VS 7: AND THE LORD GOD FORMED MAN OF THE DUST OF THE GROUND, AND BREATHED INTO HIS NOSTRILS THE BREATH OF LIFE; AND MAN BECAME A LIVING BEING. He is in us to give us the power we need to bring forth the impossible. He did not create us by mistake. He was finishing the beginning of us in His image, to become one with Him yet in our fleshly body. SO GOD CREATED MAN IN HIS OWN IMAGE; IN THE IMAGE OF GOD HE CREATED HIM; MALE AND FEMALE HE CREATED THEM. GENESIS 1 VS 27

We already have in us what we need to get to Zion. We are His people and our destiny is tied to Him. It is time for new things to come forth and birth life from those things that was once dead because hell invaded us.

PSALMS 48 VS 12: WALK ABOUT ZION, AND GO ALL AROUND HER. COUNT HER TOWERS; PSALMS 48 VS 14: FOR THIS IS GOD, OUR GOD FOREVER AND EVER; HE WILL BE OUR GUIDE EVEN TO DEATH.

As I shifted and transformed into my new man, an inner voice spoke to me "you can't walk the same walk, you can't talk the same talk and you can't keep the same company. You are now walking out of darkness into the marvelous light. Once you walk into Zion you must begin to renew your mind."

There are many scriptures which state that once you change your life or in order to change your life you have to change your mind.

***EPHESIANS 4 VS 17: THIS I SAY, THEREFORE, AND TESTIFY IN THE LORD, THAT YOU SHOULD NO LONGER WALK AS THE REST OF THE GENTILES WALK, IN THE FUTILITY OF THEIR <u>MIND</u>, HAVING THEIR UNDERSTANDING DARKENED, BEING ALIENATED FROM THE LIFE OF GOD, BECAUSE OF THE IGNORANCE THAT IS IN THEM, BECAUSE OF THE BLINDNESS OF THEIR HEART.
***EPHESIANS4 VS 21-24: IF INDEED YOU HAVE HEARD HIM AND HAVE BEEN TAUGHT BY HIM, AS THE TRUTH IS IN JESUS: THAT YOU PUT OFF, CONCERNING YOUR FORMER CONDUCT, THE OLD MAN WHICH GROWS CORRUPT ACCORDING TO THE DECIETFUL LUSTS, AND BE RENEWED IN THE SPIRIT OF YOUR <u>MIND AND THAT YOU PUT ON THE NEW MAN WHICH WAS CREATED ACCORDING TO GOD</u> IN TRUE RIGHTEOUSNESS AND HOLINESS.

***EHESIANS 5 VS 8-9:__ FOR YOU WERE ONCE <u>DARKNESS</u> BUT NOW YOU ARE LIGHT IN THE LORD. WALK AS CHILDREN OF LIGHT; (FOR THE FRUIT OF THE SPIRIT IS IN ALL GOODNESS, RIGHTEOUSNESS, AND TRUTH),
***<u>ROMANS 12 VS 2:</u> AND DO NOT BE CONFORMED TO THIS WORLD, BUT BE TRANSFORMED BY THE RENEWING OF YOUR <u>MIND</u>.

So I began to change my way of thinking hourly, daily, and nightly. I constantly meditated on the things that were good, of love and righteousness. Do you know what happened? The enemy began to try to play with my mind. He wanted me to think I was not worthy of God's love and mercy. He wanted me to think I could never be a different person from what I used to be.

As I continued to walk to Zion a voice said, "Cover yourself and put on the whole armor because you are no longer fighting physically against the world. You are now standing on spiritual battle fields."

<u>EPHESIANS 6 VS 11-20:</u> PUT ON THE WHOLE ARMOR OF GOD THAT YOU MAY BE ABLE TO STAND AGAINST THE WILES OF THE DEVIL. FOR WE DO NOT WRESTLE AGAINST FLESH AND BLOOD, BUT AGAINST PRINCIPALITIES, AGAINST POWERS, AGAINST THE RULERS OF THE DARKNESS OF THIS AGE, AGAINST SPIRITUAL HOSTS OF WICKEDNESS IN THE HEAVENLY PLACES. THEREFORE TAKE UP THE WHOLE ARMOR OF GOD THAT YOU MAY BE ABLE TO WITHSTAND IN THE EVIL DAY, AND HAVING DONE ALL, TO STAND. STAND THEREFORE, HAVING GIRDED YOUR WAIST WITH TRUTH, HAVING PUT ON THE BREASTPLATE OF RIGHTEOUSNESS, AND HAVING SHOD OUR FEET WITH THE PREPARATION OF THE GOSPEL OF PEACE; ABOVE ALL, TAKING THE SHIELD OF FAITH WITH WHICH YOU WILL BE ABLE TO QUENCH ALL THE FIERY DARTS OF THE WICKED ONE. AND TAKE THE HELMET OF SALVATION, AND THE SWORD OF THE SPIRIT, WHICH IS THE WORD OF GOD; PRAYING ALWAYS WITH ALL PRAYER AND SUPPLICATION IN THE SPIRIT, BEING WATCHFUL TO THE END WITH ALL PERSEVERANCE AND SUPPLICATION FOR ALL THE SAINTS—AND FOR ME, THAT UTTERANCE MAY BE GIVEN TO ME THAT I MAY OPEN MY MOUTH BOLDLY TO MAKE KNOWN THE MYSTERY OF THE GOSPEL, FOR WHICH I AM AN AMBASSADOR IN CHAINS; THAT IN IT I MAY SPEAK BOLDLY, AS I OUGHT TO SPEAK

I continued to walk to Zion. I pressed my way through some tough battles and rocky roads. I embraced everything God sent my way. I began to see a new me. I was able to understand God's reasons and purpose for the things I went through as a child and the things that was happening in my life.

Understandings lead me to a place of perfect peace. No matter what was going on around me, or to me, I stood strong. Not only did I stand, but I stood in the presence of God with his perfect peace that surpassed all understanding.

Every time things seemed overbearing I would here my grandmother's voice saying "God won't put more on you than you can bear". I began to hear a melody in my mind she used to love "no one told you the road would be easy, but I don't believe he brought me this far to leave me." (Mary, Mary)

I continued to walk! Staying on the path of righteousness! I held on to my destiny, and I would not let it go! I did not leave it in anyone else's hands, but God's. Only he holds power over me, because it was Him who gave me life & allowed me to become truly free.

"Continue your journey to Zion and around Zion, so you can walk in Zion on earth. Never allow a road block to stop you, for you have something more powerful on your side. Continue to press until you reach the road full of open doors and a clear mind."

Thank God! There is no more fighting playing in my mind from the iron fist. No more seeing the replay of my mother being drug up the pavement. No more seeing the bodies in the streets. No more fighting with the world or in me. No more being the enemy to my King for now I am an heir to the throne and He is facing me.

Now I can see the good times and the love my mom had for me. I can remember the laughter and the joy I had between the pains, I can see that my mom tried to do the best she could with what knowledge she had. I can see the man from the other room was in his own pain and did not know how to correct his pain so he gave out pain. Now I am able to love other's for who they are and love the God in them. I am able to understand I am who I am and that my darkness created love, knowledge, wisdom and faith. I was able to move past the things that was barricading me from my destiny.

I commanded the noise to cease! I commanded the fighting to be! I commanded the storms to leave! So, I could enter into my dreams and allow my eyes to truly see how this world tried to destroy me!

Now I am much wiser. I am much stronger. I am so much better. I am smarter! My heart feels safe and secure! I can see much clearer. I have become an angel; God would want to represent His kingdom.

Thank God my inner man was rescued from the snares of the enemy. I found out Jesus was some kin to me in spirit and in truth. By His blood, my life gained new meaning. By His act of selflessness our souls are redeemed, and we were given a chance to empty out the worldly mess to become truly free!

Now I have my crown. I am walking in favor with the anointing of God flowing around, through and in me! I ask and I receive, I seek and I find, I knock and doors are opened! No matter how much I have fallen, no matter how much pain I have encountered. No matter how much the enemy stole from me, no matter how many tricks the enemy has played he still couldn't take my destiny. The breath held on to me!

*****Break the shackles and chains that wrap around your inner man. Set your mind free so that you can step into your destiny. Empty your soul so the weight of the world is no more. Become your own knight in shining armor! Speak it! Believe it! See it! Think great thoughts because you know you where created by a great God! Take time to heal your soul! Write down everything that's hurting you, everything you are mad at, and everything that has you bound. Put everything on a list that is holding you back. Your pain and misery should be the first thing to leave. Then burn the paper and remember it no more! The fire can't burn you on those things that tried to destroy you! Zion awaits you! I'll see you there!

CHAPTER EIGHT

WHO'S YOUR DADDY NOW!

HOW CAN THE WIND BLOW AND YOU FEEL THE BREEZE BUT NOT KNOW IT IS ME! ONLY I HOLD THE MYSTERIES OF LIFE IN MY BOSOM, SO LISTEN FOR MY VOICE AND YOU WILL BEGIN TO KNOW I AM THAT MAN!

FREE YOUR MIND, EMPTY YOUR SOUL AND COME ALIVE! GOD HAS FOUND YOU AND DUSTED YOU OFF NOW DESTINY AWAITS YOU!

ISIAH 9 VS 6: **FOR UNTO US A CHILD IS BORN, UNTO US A SON IS GIVEN; AND THE GOVERNMENT WILL BE UPON HIS SHOULDER. AND HIS NAME WILL BE CALLED WONDERFUL, COUNSELOR, MIGHTY GOD, EVERLASTING FATHER, PRINCE OF PEACE.** I used to wonder why my daddy didn't continue being such a great daddy. I wondered if he still loved me, or cared for me as he did when I was born. He saw me take my first steps, say my first words and he carried me around with him like I was his pride and joy. I couldn't understand how he became mentally ill shortly after my mother took us and left. Maybe that played a part. I just don't know! But, I conditioned myself not to cry over spilt milk, so I acted like I didn't care, anyway. Those actions caused issues beyond my understanding, until I found out the truth.

The truth is God does everything for a reason. I believe He released a piece of Him in us to carry out something awesome for His glory on earth. We are apart of one body made up by many spirits of God. The problem we hold is lack of knowledge of who we really are and what our sole purpose here is. We allow the issue of our daddy being absent from our life to weigh in our mind. We leave space for the enemy to get in, and cause a constant disturbance in our heart. I truly believe this was one of the greatest tricks the enemy came up with to play with the mind and knock kids off their paths. he did this to make us feel unworthy or less of a person.

Once he realized that, he used it as a pawn to keep us in his web. It allowed pain to be planted in our mind, the minds of our children and in us as children of the kingdom. It began to become our heart aches and down falls.

The world doesn't help by implying in order for us to grow up productive and with a greater chance of being successful; we need a two parent household. Our father and mother needs to be in our lives. I will never dispute this! I just believe, what God has for us it is for us, and man can't take it away unless we let him. For some reason God did not want or need that particular person to play a part in our up bringing. Who are we to question Him! God knew who ever is missing from our life (mom or dad) had nothing to offer in the process of creating us in His image other than their genes and spiritual combinations. God only needed that person flesh genetics to create what would bring forth in us that which is needed for our spirit and our walk as we journey to our destiny.

God genetically puts two people (chosen specifically by Him) together for the sole purpose of the creation of an awesome being that will carry out a great purpose for Him. It's just hard for us to accept that one of the drivers who help bring us to this destination called earth would not continue the ride on our journey called life.

We really want that person to play apart in our lives because he played apart in our landing here on planet earth. We wonder why we were not worthy of this man or woman being apart of our lives. We question God secretly! He knows what's best. We just have to learn to trust Him.

This used to play apart in me. I felt as if I needed a man to fill the empty space in my heart that was left when my daddy no longer dwelled there. Isn't it funny, we are filled with so much mess and pain as we walk in the world, but we still feel empty inside with many voids, and when we are emptied we are full of all of God's promises?

Was it my daddy's fault: As I grew up I felt voids due to my daddy not being in my life; at least that's what I thought it came from but it didn't. I realized after many life experiences that the voids I held inside were there because I was not in tune with my true blood line. Once I became connected to my true Father (my creator), He began to fill those voids. Why would you deprive yourself because of someone else's issues? Did you ever think that God needed those people to create you, but not to raise you? He wanted to be your developer and your rock! What else do you need? God has it all! That man/woman has done its job it is up to you to find out who you are and what part of God's master plan were you sent here to carry out.

We are loaned to our parents from God! They give us what they have to give and then we are left to find the One who has the rest. We may go through things we felt broke us. It was only there to strengthen us and prepare us for higher levels in God here on earth. They (the parents) planted the seed God needed from them. Now it's time for us to find God, so he can order the steps for the rest of our life. These are the things we must instill in our sons and daughters as they grow up.

I realized even though my biological father was not really in my life much after I turned ten, and the man that was there had caused a painful shift in the grounds I walked on, I still had a Father who soon became my Daddy.

My true and real daddy was and always is God (my creator). He breathed in me and formed me in His image! His spiritual image! The inner man! My soul! This lies within me and keeps me connected to my true blood line. My true genetics is held bound by the breath my Daddy breathed in me, even when I was yet in the world scattered. By His breath I was there on the cross as Jesus took His last breath finishing the beginning of my destiny. **HEBREW 12 VS 2: LOOKING UNTO JESUS, THE AUTHOR AND FINISHER OF OUR FAITH, WHO FOR THE JOY THAT WAS SET BEFORE HIM, ENDURED THE CROSS, DESPISING THE SHAME, AND HAS SAT DOWN AT THE RIGHT HAND OF THE THRONE OF GOD.**

<u>REAL TALK</u>: There is only one Father that will give us everything we need to conquer our destiny and He is the only one worthy of that name. **MATHEW 23 VS 9: "DO NOT CALL ANYONE ON EARTH YOUR FATHER, FOR ONE IS YOUR FATHER, HE WHO IS IN HEAVEN."**

In the Webster dictionary <u>father hood means; beget; originate, pass as father or author of, act as father to; fix the paternity of.</u> ONLY GOD CAN DO AND BE ALL OF THAT! **PSALMS 68 VS 5: A FATHER OF THE FATHERLESS, A DEFENDER OF WIDOWS, IS GOD IN HIS HOLY HABITATION.**

I was held together and formed into an awesome spiritual being despite of my pain, my afflictions, my adversities and despite of my past. I became a being where when God spoke and I finally heard him, His word would form in my belly and manifest that which He spoke over my life. With His word He chastised me, and corrected me, and created in me a clean heart. He brought to me life one on one in the lions den, in the fiery furnace of hell until I found my way back to Him! **HEBREWS 12 VS 5-6: AND YOU HAVE FORGOTTEN THE EXHORTATION WHICH SPEAKS TO YOU AS TO SONS: "MY SON, DO NOT DESPISE THE CHASTENING OF THE LORD, NOR BE DISCOURAGED WHEN YOU ARE REBUKED BY HIM; FOR WHOM THE LORD LOVES HE CHASTENS, AND SCOURGES EVERY SON WHOM HE RECEIVES."**

We try to define ourselves by our worldly daddy or parents in general. I now define myself by my real daddy, my spiritual Father. By the words He spoke over me before I entered and exited the womb. Because of that I can now be me! I can now be free! Even though the enemy had me thinking I couldn't. Now I truly believe if we are equipped with the right knowledge and understanding nothing could stop us, but ourselves no matter what the situation or circumstances may be.

My father rescued me. He found me in a dark dreary corner dying. My eyes couldn't see what was in front of me. He picked me up and dusted me off and told me "you are no longer lost, just continue to pray and things will soon change." He became my eyes and ears; allowing me to see things beyond the physical eyes. **MATHEW 6 VS 9-13: "IN THIS MANNER, THEREFORE, PRAY: OUR FATHER IN HEAVEN, HALLOWED BE YOUR NAME, YOUR KINGDOM COME, YOUR WILL BE DONE ON EARTH AS IT IS IN HEAVEN. GIVE US THIS DAY OUR DAILY BREAD. AND FORGIVE US OUR DEBTS, AS WE FORGIVE OUR DEBTORS. AND DO NOT LEAD US INTO TEMPTATION, BUT DELIVER US FROM THE EVIL ONE. FOR YOURS IS THE KINGDOM AND THE POWER AND THE GLORY FOREVER. AMEN.** My spiritual daddy can give to me far more abundantly the things from and of the kingdom here on earth, than a man living in the flesh.

! I DON'T KNOW ABOUT YOU BUT ONE THING I KNOW IS WHO'S MY DADDY!

2ND **CORINTHIANS 6 VS 18: "I WILL BE A FATHER TO YOU, AND YOU SHALL BE MY SONS AND DAUGHTERS, SAYS THE LORD ALMIGHTY."** God allows us to make mistakes even though sometimes those mistakes cause us to go in circles. Once we run out of self and have no place else to run, there He is! Waiting with His hand stretched out, knowing it's time. My daddy!

He is powerful beyond a measure, that's why I am. He gave to me His breath and allowed me to see that He will always be apart of me. He left something in me so that I can give life to others and wipe tears from their eyes. My daddy has the greatest love of them all resting inside of me. He loves me unconditionally! He provides all my needs according to His riches and glory. He is my source and supply and He wipes every tear from my eyes, and numbers them for greater surprises for my future life.

My daddy forgave me for being His enemy and making those bad decisions! He forgot about my past, when I repented of my sins. He renewed my mind, after setting it free. He placed His armor around me and put my enemies under my feet.

My daddy showed me He will climb the highest mountains and part any sea to rescue me. He placed my feet on higher grounds and commanded the enemy to step down. He carried me through my hard times and gave me light, when my darkness would not shine. He allowed my soul to be set free. He saved me!

My daddy gave His only begotten son to die for me, so I can step out of captivity. **JOHN 3 VS 16: FOR GOD SO LOVED THE WORLD HE GAVE HIS ONLY BEGOTTEN SON THAT WHO SO EVER BELIEVES IN HIM SHOULD NOT PERISH BUT HAVE EVERLASTING LIFE. EHESIANS 4 VS 8: THEREFORE HE SAYS: "WHEN HE ASCENDED ON HIGH, HE LED CAPTIVITY CAPTIVE, AND GAVE GIFTS TO MEN."** Not only did He die, but after His spirit left His body He went to the lower parts of the earth. He took back the keys and released spiritual gifts to His people on earth. **EHESIANS 4 VS 9: (NOW THIS, HE ASCENDED"—WHAT DOES IT MEAN BUT THAT HE ALSO FIRST DESCENDED INTO THE LOWER PARTS OF THE EARTH?).**

My daddy loves me! He allows me to speak with Him and hear His voice. He gives me words to stand strong, so that I can hear the melody of His love song. My daddy lets me rest in His arm. When I feel a mighty storm He whispers "be still." He keeps me safe and secure! He holds me near as I walk through the valleys of the shadows of death. My daddy, He never left me! He's my protector! He's my healer! He's my comforter! He's my provider! He taught me how to love and how to care for all, even my enemies when they fall.

~~~ Do you need a daddy? I don't mind sharing mine! He's waiting to be all that you need. My daddy has enough power to take care of you and me. He is strong enough to pick us up and dust us off. He will forgive you, no doubt! He will give you all new things starting from the inside finishing on the out!

My daddy will set your mind free, and lead you out of captivity. He will give you the keys to your wildest dreams. He will help you empty your soul, and remember your mistakes no more. He is not like man. He doesn't hold your past against you. He moves past that, and waits for you. He allows your past to stay dead, when you ask him to forgive. He allows you to live beyond your errors into your destiny. Just know that He is able no matter how things seem. Just keep pressing forward and don't look back! In the Bible there is a story where God told a man name Lot that no one with him should look back, his wife looked back. **GENESIS 19 VS 26: BUT HIS WIFE LOOKED BACK BEHIND HIM, AND SHE BECAME A PILLAR OF SALT. 2ND CHRONICLES 25 VS 8: "BUT IF YOU GO, BE GONE! BE STRONG IN BATTLE! EVEN SO GOD SHALL MAKE YOU FALL BEFORE THE ENEMY; FOR GOD HAS POWER TO HELP AND TO OVERTHROW."**

Seek out your real daddy and don't look back! There is no need to cry anymore! Your biological daddy may not be there, but our father in heaven will wipe every tear from your eyes. There is no need to feel as if you are not loved by a man; evidently he wasn't designed to play a part in your upbringing, anyway just your journey to life not through life.

***So I ask why you need any other daddy if you have one like mine. He is awesome and has every thing you need at His spoken word. Let there be light and it was light; and it was good. You can find this in the book of Genesis; in the Bible. God spoke the word and it was so; God is one with you from the breath He breathed in you! You can speak the word and by faith and the power of belief it is done. How powerful is my Daddy! <u>He that is in me is greater than he that is in the world!!</u>

~~~~God wants to be your molder, your developer, your teacher, and your daddy. He wants the glory for your success, so people can know He is still God! Let Him shine so the world can shine more. Empty your soul! Let God be your daddy, your father, your every thing. He will take you to your destiny! You will begin to experience a mind set that will allow the manifestation of you words and thoughts to come into existence.

CHAPTER NINE

FROM A TO Z
MEDITATE ON THESE THINGS......

I LEAVE YOU WORDS OF WISDOM AND ENCOURAGEMENT FROM MY HEART AND SOUL. CONTINUE TO FEED YOUR MIND AND EMPTY YOUR SOUL! SPOKEN TO ME FROM GOD AND APROVED BY THE KINGDOM THAT LIVES INSIDE OF ME! (HEAVEN HAS AWAKENED IN ME!)

PHILIPPIANS 4 VS 7-8: AND THE PEACE OF GOD, WHICH SURPASSES ALL UNDERSTANDING, WILL GUARD YOUR HEARTS AND MINDS THROUGH CHRIST JESUS. FINALLY, BRETHREN, WHAT EVER THINGS ARE TRUE, WHATEVER THINGS ARE NOBLE, WHATEVER THINGS ARE JUST, WHATEVER THINGS ARE PURE, WHATEVER THINGS ARE LOVELY, WHATEVER THINGS ARE OF GOOD REPORT, IF THERE IS ANY VIRTUE AND IF THERE IS ANYTHING PRAISEWORTHY-MEDITATE ON THESE THINGS.

MAKE IT PERSONAL FOR YOU! FEED YOURSELF, TREAT YOURSELF, AND DON'T BEAT YOURSELF! IN ORDER TO RECEIVE DELIVERANCE YOU HAVE TO RECEIVE WHAT'S BEING DELIVERED TO YOU. KEEP YOUR EYES OPEN AND YOUR EARS ON SPIRITUAL GROUNDS. FIRST JUDGE YOURSELF BEFORE YOU PUT ANYONE ELSE DOWN. ALWAYS REMEMBER, **MATTHEW 7 VS 1: "JUDGE NOT, THAT YOU BE NOT JUDGED".** REMEMBER IF YOU FREE THE MIND YOU WILL EMPTY YOUR SOUL AND THE REST WILL SURELY FOLLOW.

A = ACCEPT AND ACKNOWLEDGE WHO YOU ARE, WHO GOD IS, AND WHERE HE CAN TAKE YOU. **PROVERBS 3 VS 6: IN ALL YOUR WAYS ACKNOWLEDGE HIM, AND HE SHALL DIRECT YOUR PATHS.** AFTER YOU HAVE DONE ALL TO STAND, STAND SOME MORE; EVENTUALLY YOU WILL GAIN ENOUGH STRENGTH, SO NOTHING CAN KNOCK YOU DOWN.

B = BELIEVE THAT LIMITS ARE ONLY SET IN YOUR MIND. GOD SAID "THERE ARE NO LIMITS, HE IS LIMITLESS." WE LIMIT GOD WITH LACK OF FAITH AND OUR MIND SET. I BELIEVE WE SET OUR OWN LIMITS, BUT WITH FAITH THE IMPOSSIBLE IS POSSIBLE. **HEBREWS 11 VS 6: BUT WITHOUT FAITH IT IS IMPOSSIBLE TO PLEASE HIM, FOR HE WHO COMES TO GOD MUST BELIEVE <u>THAT HE IS</u>, AND THAT HE IS A REWARDER OF THOSE WHO DILIGENTLY SEEK HIM.**

C = COURAGE GIVES YOU THE STRENGTH YOU NEED TO CHANGE YOUR MIND SO THAT YOU CAN CHANGE YOUR LIFE. **DEUTERONOMY 31 VS 6: "BE STRONG AND OF GOOD COURAGE,**

DO NOT FEAR NOR BE AFRAID OF THEM, FOR THE LORD YOUR GOD, HE IS THE ONE WHO GOES WITH YOU. HE WILL NOT LEAVE YOU NOR FORSAKE YOU."

D = DENY SELF AND DEPEND ON OUR CREATOR FOR DIRECTIONS; HE WILL WALK YOU OUT OF VALLEY LOWS AND ON TO MOUNTAIN HIGHS. **MATHEW 16 VS 24: THEN JESUS SAID TO HIS DISCIPLES, "IF ANYONE DESIRES TO GO AFTER ME LET HIM DENY HIMSELF. AND TAKE UP HIS CROSS, AND FOLLOW ME.**

E = EXCEL BEYOND YOUR CIRCUMSTANCES IN DARKNESS AND COMMAND YOUR FLESH TO FALL TO BRING LIGHT. **ECCLESIASTES 2 VS 13: THEN I SAW THAT WISDOM EXCELS FOLLY AS LIGHT EXCELS DARKNESS.**

F = FORGET THE THINGS THAT LIE BEHIND YOU AND CONQUER YOUR PRESENT ISSUES. FEED YOUR MIND, BODY, AND SOUL THE PROPER FOODS TO GROW. **PHILIPPIANS 3 VS 13: BRETHREN I DO NOT COUNT MYSELF TO HAVE APPREHENDED; BUT ONE THING I DO, FORGETTING THOSE THINGS WHICH ARE BEHIND AND REACHING FORWARD TO THOSE THINGS WHICH ARE AHEAD.**

G = GREATER IS HE THAT IS IN ME THAN HE THAT IS IN THE WORLD! GOD CAN SUPPLY ALL YOUR NEEDS IF YOU JUST KNOW HIS GREATNESS. **PHILIPPIANS 4 VS 19 AND MY GOD SHALL SUPPLY ALL YOUR NEEDS ACCORDING TO HIS RICHES IN GLORY BY CHRIST JESUS.**

H = HERE YOU HAVE A CITIZENSHIP IN HEAVEN AND THE WORLD CAN'T TAKE IT AWAY, UNLESS YOU GIVE UP YOUR BIRTHRIGHTS, TO IT. **PHILIPPIANS 3 VS 20: FOR OUR CITIZENSHIP IS IN HEAVEN, FROM WHICH WE ALSO EAGERLY WAIT FOR THE SAVIOR, THE LORD JESUS CHRIST,**

I = I WILL NEVER GIVE UP 7 MINUTES BEFORE THE BREAK THROUGH! **PHILIPPIANS 4 VS 6: BE ANXIOUS FOR NOTHING, BUT IN EVERYTHING BY PRAYER AND SUPPLICATIONS, WITH THANKSGIVING, LET YOUR REQUESTS BE MADE KNOWN TO GOD.** IN YOUR MIND YOU CAN BRING FORTH LIFE AS YOU DESIRE IT TO UNFOLD. IN DUE TIME IT WILL MANIFEST, IF YOU DON'T LET GOD GO!

J = JUSTICE STANDS IN THE HANDS OF THE ONE THAT CHANGES THE LAW OF OPPOSITION WITHIN THEIR MIND AND THOUGHTS. (U.REED) I AM JUSTIFIED BY FAITH. **ROMANS 3 VS 28: THEREFORE WE CONCLUDE THAT A MAN IS JUSTIFIED BY FAITH APART FROM THE DEEDS OF THE LAW.**

K = KNOWLEDGE IS POWER; IF YOU GAIN KNOWLEDGE YOU GAIN POWER. GAINING KNOWLEDGE= KNOWLEDGE OF TRIBULATION WHICH PRODUCES PERSEVERANCE; AND PERSEVERANCE, CHARACTER; AND CHARACTER, HOPE AND HOPE FAITH TO WITHSTAND. **ROMANS 5 VS 5: NOW HOPE DOES NOT DISAPPOINT, BECAUSE THE LOVE OF GOD HAS BEEN POURED OUT IN OUR HEARTS BY THE HOLY SPIRIT WHO WAS GIVEN TO US.** THE HOLY SPIRIT HELPS YOU GAIN POWER. WHY NOT TRY HIM AND SEE.

L = **LET GO AND LET GOD! LET HIM LOVE YOU AND YOU LOVE THYSELF!** THE GREATEST LOVE YOU WILL EVER CONQUER IS WHAT YOU FIND BURIED DOWN UNDERNEATH THE REBELS OF PAIN. (U.REED) JUST LET GO AND SEE WHAT YOU FIND. **1ST CORINTHIANS 13 VS 4-7 & 13: LOVE SUFFERS LONG AND IS KIND; LOVE DOES NOT ENVY; LOVE DOES NOT PARADE ITSELF, IS NOT PUFFED UP; DOES NOT BEHAVE RUDELY, DOES NOT SEEK ITS OWN, IS NOT PROVOKED, THINKS NO EVIL; DOES NOT REJOICE IN INIQUITY, BUT REJOICES IN THE TRUTH; BEARS ALL THINGS, ENDURES ALL THINGS. VS 13: AND NOW ABIDE FAITH, HOPE, LOVE, THESE THREE; BUT THE GREATEST OF THESE IS LOVE.**

M = MASTER THE ABILITY TO OPEN DOORS WITH YOUR MIND BY TAPPING INTO THE WALLS OF DIVINITY THAT LIE IN YOUR SOUL. DON'T ALLOW THE SEEN TO STOP THE UNSEEN. (U.REED) **2ND CORINTHIANS 5 VS 7: FOR WE WALK BY FAITH NOT BY SIGHT. 2ND CORINTHIANS 4 VS 18: WHILE WE DO NOT LOOK AT THE THINGS WHICH ARE SEEN, BUT AT THE THINGS WHICH ARE NOT SEEN. FOR THE THINGS WHICH ARE SEEN ARE TEMPORARY, BUT THE THINGS WHICH ARE NOT SEEN ARE ETERNAL.**

N = NEVER ALLOW YESTERDAYS' WORRIES TO AFFECT YOUR TOMORROW. IT TAKES AWAY THE STRENGTH YOU NEED FOR TODAY! (U.REED) **MATTHEW 6 VS 34: "THEREFORE DO NOT WORRY ABOUT TOMORROW, FOR TOMORROW WILL WORRY ABOUT ITS OWN THINGS. SUFFICIENT FOR THE DAY IS ITS OWN TROUBLE."**

O = OPERATE WITHIN THE GROUNDS OF OBEDIENCE TO OVER COME OBSTACLES, AND OPEN DOORS YOU HAVE ASKED FOR FROM GOD. **MATTHEW 7 VS 7: "ASK, AND IT WILL BE GIVEN TO YOU; SEEK, AND YOU WILL FIND; KNOCK AND IT WILL BE OPENED TO YOU.**

P = PURPOSE DROVE ME INTO DESTINY, WHERE I FOUND A MAN WHO FILLED MY HEART AND DIED FOR ME. HE SET MY SOUL FREE. **THE ONLY ONE THAT CAN FULFILL YOUR HEART IS**

THE ONE THAT CREATED IT AND MADE YOU! HE BREATHED IN YOU TO LEAVE A PIECE OF HIM FOR PURPOSE AND DESTINY. TAKE THE STEPS TO EMPTY IT OUT AND LET HIM IN!

Q = QUICKLY OVERCOME AND OVERTAKE FEAR WITH THE KNOWLEDGE OF WHY IT'S THERE. IT IS THERE TO STOP YOU AND DISTRACT YOU! **ISAIAH 35 VS. 4: SAY TO THOSE WHO ARE FEARFUL-HEARTED, "BE STRONG, DO NOT FEAR! BEHOLD, YOUR GOD WILL COME WITH VENGEANCE, WITH THE RECOMPENSE OF GOD; HE WILL COME AND SAVE YOU."**

R = **REDEMPTION:** FOR I HAVE WALKED THROUGH THE FIRES OF LIFE AND CAME OUT UNBURNED ONCE I FIGURED OUT WHO LIVES IN ME. **GOD!** IN THE FIRE (STRUGGLES, AFFLICTIONS, PAIN, MISERY, TRIALS) OF MY LIFE MY SOUL WAS REDEEMED. (READ IN DANIELS 3 VS 19-30) **MESHACK, SHADRACH AND ABEDNEGO WERE PUT INTO A FIERY FURNACE FOR REFUSING TO BOW DOWN TO AN IDOL OF GOLD. THEY CAME OUT UNBURNED AND UNAFFECTED. NOT EVEN THE SMELL OF SMOKE ON THEIR BODY OR GARMENTS. REAL FAITH HELPS YOU STAND IN FIRE AND NOT GET BURNED!**

S = **SALVATION**: WHO IS WORTH LOSING THAT WHICH JESUS HAS ALREADY PAID THE PRICE FOR? ONCE YOU UNDERSTAND THIS, YOU MUST SURRENDER, SACRIFICE YOURSELF, LET GO OF THE WORLD AND HOLD ON TO GOD'S UNCHANGING HANDS. **PSALMS 118 VS 14-15: THE LORD IS MY STRENGTH AND SONG, AND HE HAS BECOME MY SALVATION. THE VOICE OF REJOICING AND SALVATION IS IN THE TENTS OF THE RIGHTEOUS; THE RIGHT HAND OF THE LORD DOES VALIANTLY.**

T = THUGS CRY TOO! PEOPLE NEED TO KNOW WE ARE ALL APART OF ONE BODY. WE NEED TO CONQUER THE INNER DEMONS AND SET OUR SOULS FREE. WHEN WE ACCEPT AND REALIZE WE ARE WHOM WE ARE, WE WILL REALIZE JESUS SAVED US ALL ALLOWING US TO BECOME A NEW MAN TO FORM ONE BODY. (U.REED) THANK GOD WE ALL CAN BE CHANGED! **MATHEW 17 VS 18: AND JESUS REBUKED THE DEMON, AND IT CAME OUT OF HIM; AND THE CHILD WAS CURED FROM THAT VERY HOUR. **KNOW THY SELF! TO THYSELF BE TRUE! NOW FIND THE NEW YOU!**

U = **UNDERSTANDING**-WE NEED IT! WITHOUT IT YOU ARE FORCED INTO A PLACE WHERE YOU STAGNATE YOUR STEPS, AND LOSE THE PLACE IN YOUR MIND WHERE YOUR DIVINE ORDER STANDS. **PROVERBS 14 VS 8: THE WISDOM OF THE PRUDENT IS TO UNDERSTAND HIS WAY, BUT FOLLY OF FOOLS IS DECEIT.**

V = VISIBLE DOES NOT MEAN ACTUAL. INVISIBLE MEANS POSSIBLE. YOUR WORLDLY EYES CAN PLAY TRICKS

ON YOUR INNER SOUL IF YOU DON'T UNDERSTAND THAT THE GREATEST THINGS ARE INVISIBLE. (U.REED) **COLOSSIANS 3 VS 2-3: SET YOUR MIND ON THINGS ABOVE, NOT ON THINGS ON THE EARTH. FOR YOU DIED, AND YOUR LIFE IS HIDDEN WITH CHRIST IN GOD. SO ONCE YOU FIND CHRIST YOU FIND YOUR TRUE LIFE.**

W = WE HAVE BEEN CALLED TO STILL WATERS. THERE WE WILL SEE OUR REFLECTIONS CLEARLY, AS WE EMPTY OUR SOULS. THE HOLY SPIRIT IS OUR SPIRITUAL WATER THAT CONSUMES OUR BODIES. **PSALMS 46 VS 10: BE STILL AND KNOW THAT I AM GOD.**

X = **EXAMINE** THAT WHICH THE WORLD MADE YOU. SEARCH FOR WHAT GOD (CREATOR) PREDESTINED YOU TO BECOME. YOUR LIFE MAY OR MAY NOT BE HELD IN SHACKLES AND CHAINS, BUT IF YOUR MIND ISN'T FREE YOU'RE NOT FREE. **(U.REED)** **1ST CORINTHIANS 11 VS 28: BUT LET A MAN EXAMINE HIMSELF, AND SO LET HIM EAT OF THE BREAD AND DRINK OF THE CUP.**

Y = YESTERDAY IS WHAT YOU WALKED OUT OF TRYING TO FIND TODAY, WHY WOULD YOU LOOK BACK TRYING TO FIGURE OUT TOMORROW, WHEN YOUR EYES ARE ALREADY SET FOR NOW! **(U.REED)** DON'T LOOK BACK, DESTINY AWAITS YOU! **PSALMS 28 VS 7: IN HIS HEART A MAN PLANS HIS COURSE BUT THE LORD DETERMINES HIS STEPS.**

Z = ZIP DOWN THE OLD MAN (FLESH) AND ALLOW THE NEW MAN (THE WARRIOR) TO RISE UP AND STEP OUT INTO ZION! DON'T STOP YOUR OWN PROCESS. (U.REED) MAKE THE FIRST STEP AND GOD WILL DO THE REST. **MATTHEW 6 VS 33: "BUT SEEK FIRST THE KINGDOM OF GOD AND HIS RIGHTEOUSNESS AND ALL THESE THINGS SHALL BE ADDED TO YOU.**

***BIRTHING TAKES PLACE AT NINE MONTHS, SO I GAVE YOU NINE CHAPTERS. COME FORTH FROM THE WOMB AND TAKE BACK WHAT THE ENEMY STOLE FROM YOU. GAIN ALL THE SPIRITUAL KEYS TO OPEN UP YOUR DESTINY; THROUGH OBEDIENCE YOU GAIN: *YOUR JOY BACK, *YOUR PEACE BACK, *YOUR FAITH STRONGER!

THROUGH SACRIFICES, ADVERSITIES AND SURRENDERING YOU CAN REACH YOUR DESTINATION: HEAVEN ON EARTH! THE KINGDOM! TRUE KINGS AND QUEENS!! YOU MUST BE WILLING TO PRESS THROUGH THE WILDERNESS, DARKNESS AND PAIN.
■■

~THE ROAD TO FINDING GOD IN YOU~

0= 360 DEGREES COMPLETE CIRCLE OF LIFE

1= MERCY

2= REDEMPTION

3= PERSERVERANCE

4= UNDERSTANDING

5= KNOWLEDGE

6= WISDOM

7= GOD=ONE WITH YOU (WHICH IS THE LOVE THAT RESTS WITHIN YOU; UNCONDITIONAL LOVE COMPLETING THE CIRCLE OF LIFE FROM THE CENTER OF IT!) GOD IS THE CENTER!

*GOD IS THE CENTER OF A COMPLETE CIRCLE IN OUR LIFE, WHICH CONNECTS HIM TO EVERY PART OF US!

*IN OUR <u>CIRCLE</u> OF LIFE GOD HAS <u>MERCY</u> ON US SO WE CAN <u>REDEEM</u> OUR SOULS IN ORDER TO HELP US <u>PERSEVERE</u> ON OUR JOURNEY TO A PLACE OF <u>UNDERSTANDING</u> OPENING OUR MIND WITH THE <u>KNOWLEDGE</u> OF WHO <u>GOD</u> IS AND WHO WE TRULY ARE; RELEASING <u>WISDOM</u> CREATING OUR MIND WITH THE POWER OF <u>GOD</u> WHICH BRINGS FORTH THE TRUE MANIFESTATION OF <u>GOD</u> IN YOU!!

ONCE WE FIND HIM AS OUR CENTER HE COMPLETES US AND MAKES US WHOLE. HE ALLOWS US TO CONQUER OUR TRUE DESTINY BY OPENING UP DOORS THAT RELEASES OUR HEART'S DESIRES! THROUGH THE EMPTYING OF OUR SOUL/MIND WE FIND THAT THIS UNIVERSE IS TRULY OURS. ALLOWING US TO BECOME COMPLETE!

*WHAT ARE YOU GOING TO DO? <u>ONLY YOU CAN STOP THE RAIN, BECAUSE ONLY YOU AND GOD UNDERSTAND YOUR PAIN!</u> WHEN YOU EMPTY YOUR SOUL AND BECOME ONE WITH HIM WHO CREATED YOU, YOU OPEN UP A WORLD OF OPPORTUNITIES YOU COULDN'T SEE IN PAIN.

*** YOUR TOMORROW CAN ONLY BRING THE AFFECTS FROM YESTERDAY, IF YOU ALLOW YOUR TODAY TO BE FILLED WITH YESTERDAY'S PROBLEMS AND OTHER PEOPLE ISSUES! REDEEM YOURSELF!

SPOKEN: BY UGANDA REED

AN ANGEL'S COVERING

COVER ME WITH YOUR WINGS LEADING ME TO LIVE MY DREAMS. FOR YOUR EYES HAVE SEEN WHAT'S NEXT FOR ME, SO GUIDE ME TO MY DESTINY.

THOUGH THE WIND BLOWS, YET I'M STILL, CAUSE YOU HOLD ME NEAR. ALLOWING ME TO CONTINUE TO CLIMB THE HILLS WITHIN MY MIND.

FOR AS I JOURNEY THROUGH TIME YOU STOP ME IN MY TRACKS, TO GIVE ME TIME TO STEP BACK. ALLOWING ME TO SEE THE BEAUTY OF LIFE THROUGH YOUR EYES, AS YOU COVER ME.

EVEN THOUGH I MAY TRAVEL ROADS UNKNOWN TO MY DESTINY, YOU OPEN MY EYES SO THAT I CAN SEE AS YOU GUIDE ME THROUGH THOSE LIFE'S MYSTERIES.

LEADING ME TO MOUNTAIN TOPS FROM VALLEY LOWS, SHOUTING EVERYTHING MUST GO! EMPTYING OUT OF ME EVERYTHING GOD DIDN'T PUT IN ME; PUSHING ME TO MY DESTINY, AS YOU COVER ME WITH YOUR WINGS.

BY UGANDA REED

ZION! MY SOUL IS DANCING WITH DESTINY

IN THE WIND I SHALL BE FREE AS A SPIRIT SOARING TO ITS DESTINY.

I SHALL DANCE FREELY THROUGH THE AIR AND FIND PEACE SOMEWHERE.

WITH MY EYES CLOSED I SHALL SEE MY INNER SOUL MOVING ENDLESSLY AS A ROARING SEA.

AS I DANCE TO THE SWEET MELODY OF MY FATHER'S VOICE I SHALL FEEL THE WIND FROM HIS BREEZE, AS I CONQUER MY PURPOSE AND LIVE MY DREAMS.

SO, WHEN YOU SEE ME MOVING AS A FREE SPIRIT TOUCH ME; FROM THE HEAT YOU WILL FEEL THE RELEASE OF MY SOUL AS DESTINY UNFOLDS.

YOU WILL HEAR THE SOUND OF DESTINY FROM WITHIN, AS MY TEARS SET ME FREE, FROM THE STRUGGLES OF LIFE THAT USE TO ENTANGLE ME.

NOW I SHALL CLOSE MY EYES AND LISTEN TO THE SWEET MELODY OF ZION AS I SET MY MIND FREE, WHILE MY SOUL DANCES WITH DESTINY.

BY UGANDA REED

NOTES……

**** WRITE DOWN EVERYTHING YOU NEED TO SEND AWAY AND RELEASE THEM! WRITE DOWN WHAT YOU NEED TO LET GO AND PRAY YOUR WAY TO IT BY GOING THROUGH IT! I KNOW IT'S NOT EASY BUT YOU ALREADY HAVE IT IN YOU TO MAKE IT.

****WRITE DOWN EVERYTHING IN YOUR LIFE THAT IS CONNECTED TO GOD. THE THINGS THAT ARE NOT CONNECTED TO YOUR CREATOR CHANGE IT! HE IS WAITING TO GIVE YOU THE KINGDOM BECAUSE YOU ARE A KINGDOM'S CHILD, HERE ON EARTH THE KINGDOM IS INSIDE OF YOU! TRULY FREE YOURSELF BY FREEING YOUR MIND AND EMPTYING YOUR SOUL!

*****DRAW A CIRCLE AND PLACE GOD IN THE CENTER. CONNECT EVERYTHING YOU DESIRE, EVERYTHING THAT IS IMPORTANT TO YOU AND EVERYTHING YOU WANT GOD TO FIX; TO GOD. MEDITATE ON IT DAILY! HOURLY IF YOU CAN! SET YOUR MIND FREE!!

www.ingramcontent.com/pod-product-compliance
Lightning Source LLC
Chambersburg PA
CBHW031645040426
42453CB00006B/214